Survival of the Human Race

Bill and Dana Cave

With help from
Barbara Ann (Cave) Laber

Foundation for Survival of the Human Race

Copyright © 2009 Foundation for Survival of the Human Race
309 Morris Avenue
Spring Lake, NJ 07762

All rights reserved. No part of this book may be reproduced, in any form or by any means, without permission from the publisher.

Published by International Economic Technologies Corp., Spring Lake, NJ.

Printed in the United States of America

ISBN 0-9785245-1-7

To our family

Contents

Forward i

Introduction 1

Chapter 1: Survival 5

Chapter 2: Truth 9

Chapter 3: Consideration 21

Chapter 4: World Population Growth 27

Chapter 5: Allegiance 33

Chapter 6: History 39

Chapter 7: Measurement 49

Chapter 8: Science 57

Chapter 9: Relationships 65

Chapter 10: Governments 77

Chapter 11: Disputes 93

Chapter 12: Conclusion 101

References 105

Forward

This book is the first in a series produced by the Foundation for Survival of the Human Race (FSHR).

FSHR was founded in 1995 to perform research, and to acquire and disseminate knowledge that will aid in the survival of the human race.

FSHR carries out research on a scientific basis, free from external distorting influences, e.g. any political or financial biases. It encourages its researchers to seek all pertinent facts, and work to eliminate any possible distortion in perceptions of reality. It engages in scientific research that includes experimentation and analysis to support postulating and testing hypothesis relating to:

- Factors affecting human survival
- Cause and effect relationships affecting human survival
- Models pertaining to the probability of survival of different societies
- Relevant live and simulated experiments which are aimed at characterizing the factors affecting human survival

The Foundation has been pursuing an understanding of the underlying causes of crime, terrorism, civil unrest, revolutions, and wars. It is investigating factors that can be controlled in a positive manner to deter these hostile activities over the long term.

The Foundation is also investigating approaches to the development of models to predict what actions humans may take to prolong their survival. Part of this effort will require analysis of the relative values of goods and services across nations. This information will help the Foundation to produce quantitative measures that can be used to accurately represent relative values in models of different societies, as well as validate these models.

Survival of the Human Race

Introduction

The human race is rapidly becoming a tightly interrelated set of vastly different societies. Its survival depends upon the survival of at least one of those societies. Which ones, if any, will survive to see the next millennia, century, or decade? This may sound like a pessimistic question, but the facts are - there are many threats to our survival.

In the 1964 movie "On The Beach," the human race was wiped out by a nuclear holocaust. This was not a science fiction movie. To the contrary, it depicted a very real concern during the days of the Cold War (circa 1946-1989), when both the U.S. and Russia were following a Mutually Assured Destruction (MAD) policy. If one pulled the trigger, so would the other. Even back then, each had enough nuclear weapons to wipe out human life on our planet. Although the news media in the U.S. generally refrains from full disclosure on this topic, the situation is more real today. The amount of destruction that can be unleashed by a single bomb can cause fall-out that would be catastrophic for some fraction of the earth's population. However, the number of nuclear weapons currently in the hands of a single small nation can cause a nuclear holocaust that could wipe out most of the human race, see Hirsch[1].

Nuclear weapons are just one of the threats to the human race. However, based upon current scientific knowledge, it is by far the most immediate concern. But, we must consider others, such as unfamiliar diseases, other weapons of mass destruction, e.g., biological or chemical agents, or unforeseeable changes in our universe that could affect planet earth and wipe out the human race. But more importantly, we must consider those underlying problems over whose solutions we have control - problems that may lead directly to our own self-destruction.

Survival of the Human Race

What will it take to ensure our survival as we move further into the future? This question is addressed here as: What must the collective societies making up the human race do to maximize their likelihood of survival as far into the future as possible?

In this book we offer two principles that provide the basis for maximizing our chances of survival. These two principles are *Truth* and *Consideration*. To make use of these principles requires establishing a firm understanding of them based upon definitions that are clear and logically consistent. This requires a careful distinction between fact and opinion.

The reason we must be able to distinguish between fact and opinion is to be able to uncover reality - the *truth*. While some people seek the truth, others work to hide it - to protect immediate or selfish interests. Those who work to hide the truth prefer to cloud issues with emotional appeals, contriving to push unproven theories that suit their special interests. However, within any society, those individuals who have an accurate perspective of reality are in the best position to deal with the issues they face. They will be able to use truth to make the best judgments based upon reality. Consequently, those with the best judgment naturally have a higher probability of being a survivor.

Conversely, one cannot survive alone. One must depend upon relationships with others to combat the difficulties of survival when the going gets tough. Relationships that hold up under dire circumstances depend upon bonds of trust and consideration. Will the other person treat me fairly? Will they be considerate - as in the golden rule?

The theme of this book is that: *truth and consideration are the keys to survival.* As individuals, we must have a strong desire to seek the truth and be honest about our findings. Along with this, we must be both *willing* and *prepared* to face the truth about where we are heading. We must look beyond tomorrow and seek the paths most likely to ensure our survival. Recognition of this need is paramount as the earth effectively "shrinks" around us more rapidly every year.

Survival of the Human Race

To survive, a society must act together in a way that garners trust and respect. This implies being considerate of other people, not just in a single society, but across all societies that make up the human race. Both truth and consideration are complex principles. We have just started to scratch the surface to understand their important properties. But that is the purpose of this book - to clearly define these two basic principles and show why they are so critical to our survival.

We do not claim to have a *magic* solution for survival. As you will see throughout this book, we pose many questions that we do not attempt to answer. We offer statements of principle that we feel have stood the test of time - thousands of years of history. We encourage others to contribute additional thoughts to help our common cause.

We believe that the survivors will be those who have the fortitude to both seek and expose the truth and be considerate of their fellow humans - across the entire human race. These people will be the ones who gain the knowledge of how to survive and have the courage to use it. As history has shown, only these people will be prepared with the judgment required to make the difficult decisions, the conviction required to change direction, and the self-discipline required to improve their likelihood of survival.

And that's what this book is about.

Survival of the Human Race

Survival of the Human Race

Chapter 1: Survival

"The most important thing is to not stop questioning."
-Albert Einstein

There is no greater motivator of human behavior than survival. Our actions toward achieving survival are influenced by instincts and learning. Our instincts are genetic. Our learned capabilities depend upon the environment in which we were trained. Genetic instincts take many generations to evolve. One's learning environment can change within days, being destroyed by a powerful enemy, or by moving to a different environment. Students from all over the world are migrating to the United States to take advantage of the learning environment.

Students of archeology and anthropology learn about ancient migration paths taken by the intelligent ancestors of a society. Such migration is motivated by the desire for a better life - measured simply by a higher probability of survival.

These students also learn that survival of a species depends upon their level of reproduction. If a society is unable to reproduce sufficiently, it is doomed to extinction. This implies that societies require environments that protect their ability to reproduce, see Levy[1].

Survival also depends upon sufficient amounts of food, clothing, and shelter. Most species depend upon other species for food to survive. Without the food chain, it is not clear what would remain. Learning about such complex processes is critical to the survival of the human race.

Survival of the Human Race

There are many such processes about which we humans must be concerned. Some of us have never worried about survival, and question the time spent trying to understand our environment. But our environment is more than food, clothing, and shelter. We are affected by earthquakes, tsunamis, volcanic eruptions and other natural events over which we appear to have little control. We must seek the truth about what we can control.

Of all the factors that directly affect the human race - and our likelihood of survival - the most important is our relationships with other human beings. There are no greater dangers to human life today than the harmful behaviors that some humans inflict on others. These behaviors are typically driven by greed. Brutal treatment of innocent people or confiscation of their rightful property inevitably leads to hatred. This in turn leads to retaliation and conflict.

Conversely, there are no greater ways to eliminate dangers in general than by working together to help each other. What we must strive to understand is how we can apply our limited resources to ensure the likelihood for survival, as far into the future as possible. But this will require a quest for understanding what is best, and this involves a search for the truth. And this is why Einstein said "The most important thing is to not stop questioning."

So why have whole societies, such as the Mayas and the Incas, disappeared after having achieved a high degree of culture relative to their neighbors and counterparts? What has caused so many societies to rise and fall, come and go? Why have some societies, e.g., Russia, declined to such a low standard of living relative to the vast amounts of natural resources necessary to thrive on their own, and the technological skills to capitalize on those resources? Why do major superpowers go to war with each other?

How did Germany and Japan become so strong so fast after World War II, having been devastated by that War? Considering Japan's limited natural resources and precarious size, how did it become the world's most feared economic power during the 1980's and 1990's?

Survival of the Human Race

Why do some societies try to destroy others? Why are some societies more likely to survive than others? What are the mechanics of survival? How can we set standards to ensure maximizing survival of the human race? What will it take to ensure the long-term survival of a society?

Archeologists and anthropologists often cite the initiation and extinction of the population on Easter Island as an example of how a society grew to be strong and wealthy, only to be wiped out. The demise of such societies has largely been the result of their own actions.

Known to be uninhabited until discovered by boat people at approximately 900 AD, the people who landed on Easter Island grew to be a very well off society. They were fortunate to discover an environment that could support a great increase in population. With relatively large areas of forest and vegetation, survival was relatively easy, and the population swelled. Yet, centuries later, this growing population became extinct.

Today the boat people of Easter Island are the subject of archaeological studies on survival and extinction. We will summarize the scientific deductions. As a natural phenomenon, populations tend to grow exponentially until hitting a nonlinear barrier. In most cases this barrier is a lack of food or other commodity that a society comes to depend upon for survival. In the Easter Island case it was food.

In typical cases like this, people tend to migrate to other areas to gain access to larger stores of needed commodities. But three factors restricted this. First, Easter Island was sufficiently distant from other land areas that one had to travel by boat (about 17 days) to get there. Second, although these people arrived by boat, they never planned to leave, and had not preserved their boats. Third, they took down all of the trees, so there was no wood to construct new boats. In the end, they fought with each other to survive. Eventually the original population was wiped out, as modern day visitors took over the island.

Survival of the Human Race

In the process of learning how to survive, we must understand the concepts and importance of truth. We must learn how to discern truth and its distribution through society. We must take a hard look at our history. What is going on in the world today and what events have brought us to where we are? Does science play a role in our survival?

Obtaining truth is critical to our survival, and seeking the truth requires asking questions like those above. Some of these questions are not easily answered.

Why should a person be concerned with survival? How many people think of it as an issue? Our view is that too few people are conscious of how fragile the survival of a society may be. We want to encourage people to be aware of the importance of the role of survival in our daily lives, our nation, and our world. If we humans are in danger of becoming extinct, if the human race doesn't survive, then there isn't any need to worry about our children and grandchildren. If we really care about them, if we don't want to be part of another Easter Island, then we must try to understand the possible threats.

Survival should be a private as well as public goal. When we say private goal, we suggest that people search within to understand their desire to survive. They must learn how to survive in their communities, among friends and families. They must also learn how to help ensure the survival of our nation. As Einstein said, this requires *questioning* - particularly the words and actions of our politicians, mass media, and the government. People must be cognizant of threats to survival of the human race as well as their immediate world. Hopefully, enough individuals will comprehend our appeal and explain it to others, if not exert influence, to help make survival a common goal. With survival as a common goal, we are in a better position to help ensure survival of our communities, our nations, and the human race.

Survival of the Human Race

Chapter 2: Truth

> "I swear to tell the truth, the whole
> truth, and nothing but the truth,
> so help me God."

Truth appears to be a simple concept, but is it? It seems that people only worry about truth when they are discussing the law, investigations, police work, etc.; or in sports, when there are rule violations and close calls have to be made. More often, it seems that any information received in our daily lives is taken for granted as truth. Should we assume the information we hear is always the "truth"? What may seem like truth really may be misleading information.

Have you ever had a conversation with someone when, in the middle of it, you start to wonder if that person is telling the truth? It is likely that many of us have been in that position before. Whether or not we are consciously thinking about it, truth is very important to us. As Titus Livius said, "We fear things in proportion to our ignorance of them." In other words, if we do not try to seek and understand the truth, then we will remain ignorant and live in fear of what we do not know.

In fact, truth is essential to us; we don't like to be misled. If you find that you have been misled, you feel gullible, vulnerable, and maybe angry. Many people have the ability to mislead or deceive us: friends, significant others, co-workers, etc. But, what if news medias and governments mislead us?

Survival of the Human Race

How do we really know when someone is telling the truth? How can we tell? The *truth* is, we may not be able to! Think about all the people we come into contact with everyday and all the information that is transferred. There is no such thing as a filtration system for misleading or deceitful information. So, how does a person go about filtering information to find the truth?

Defining Truth

We begin our definition of truth by discussing the meaning of the word. According to the dictionary, the word 'true' has the following meanings: (1) being in accordance with the actual state of things; conforming to fact; not false. (2) Real or genuine. (3) Free from deceit; sincere. *Truth* is defined as *that which is true.*

Most cultures place truth as a high moral value that they expect to be taken seriously. But when we say it is important to *tell* the *truth,* what do we really mean? The full meaning of truth warrants deeper thought. A clearer understanding of what truth really is can help improve communications between people, and help resolve conflicts and misunderstandings.

We will start by considering the two sides of truth: seeking the truth and telling the truth. When *seeking* the truth, how do we know when we have found it? And, once we have found what we think is the truth, we must then be sure we are *telling* it. These both imply a clear measure of truth.

Survival of the Human Race

Seeking the Truth

To understand what's involved in seeking the truth, we will describe an experiment that you can perform with others as a game. A group of four to eight people sit around a box that holds five dice. To begin, the lid on the box is shut and the box is shaken so that the dice are jumbled. When the lid is opened, the people are asked to observe the dice and write down the values they see. This is the *observation* period.

For the first round, the lid is left open for a sufficient period of time so everyone has ample time to see the faces of the dice. Then it is shut. During this observation period, everyone writes down the values of the dice as they observed them. Then the lid is opened again until everyone agrees on the *true values*. This is the *validation* period. Once everyone agrees, round one ends.

This sequence is performed repeatedly. At the start of each new round, the box is shaken. In each successive round, the lid is left open for a shorter observation time. For example, in the second round, the observation period is 10 seconds. For the third round, the observation period is 8 seconds. For each new round, the observation period is shorter than the previous round.

As the experiment proceeds, differences grow between what is written down during the observation period and what is agreed upon during the validation period. When the lid is left open for a sufficient time for validation, all participants agree on the *true values* because the dice are readily observed. During the validation period, it is clear who did not record the true values of the dice during the observation period. In this kind of experiment, we note that some people can be consistently more accurate in their first observations of the dice, while others may not.

Survival of the Human Race

Being able to determine the *true values* of the dice depends on the length of time the box is left open, where a person is positioned, how well they are able to memorize under pressure, and so on. Until the box is open long enough to reveal the true values of the dice to everyone, not everyone knows the true values.

What occurs in this experiment represents what occurs in real life. The dice represent truth and facts, while the observers represent the people. The lid to the box represents our information channels. Who and where you are determines what kind of information you will receive. Some people are able to gather the facts, while others are not. Since people gain different information, what some people may perceive as the truth, others may not.

Understanding the simple concept that this game provides is a major step toward learning what it means to seek the truth. Our foundation would like to see everyone seeking the truth.

Perceptions of the Truth

In trying to understand the definition of truth, we have come to learn that there are two sides to it. One is seeking it. The other is telling it. Given that we have worked to seek the truth, let's consider what might be our *perceptions* of the truth.

There are many factors that go into a person's perception of the truth. Some of these factors may be: intelligence, age, where the information came from, emotional attachments, etc. Even though people believe they are telling the truth, they may not be. Instead, they are giving their *perception* of the truth.

Survival of the Human Race

In the sport of football, there are always conflicts in how one perceives the truth. When a player violates a rule, the referee must make a call. Sometimes this is difficult to do because the game is played so fast that what actually happened might not have been seen clearly. One team is yelling that the player did one thing, while the other team is yelling the complete opposite.

Once the referee makes a call, if it does not favor the team for which a person is cheering, they will probably disagree with the referee's decision and be very upset. So, how do we know what the *truth* is? In football today, it is easier to find out because games are recorded. The team opposing what is considered a bad call can request the referee to play back the tape to see what actually happened, in other words to determine the *real* truth. The next time you are watching a sporting event, take the time to observe how people perceive the truth differently. Do they seem to perceive truth more often in favor of the team they are cheering for, while the referees try to make the fairest call based on what they perceived to be true?

What happens during a game of football happens everywhere in life. Everyone has heard the well-known saying "there are always two sides to a story." Quoting Foster Meharny Russel, "Every story has three sides to it - yours, mine, and the facts." This is probably closer to reality. Different people have different perceptions of events in life and pass these perceptions on to others. Different perceptions of an event being passed from person to person can cause further misperceptions, making it hard to determine the truth.

These difficulties arise from what in science is termed *perception* or *measurement* error. The football example shows the difference between perceptions and reality. Reality, or truth, is what actually occurred. Our perceptions come from what we are able to observe, whether or not it is true, and built-in biases toward remembering what we want to remember, based upon our own personal history.

Survival of the Human Race

Ground Truth

When seeking the truth, we are often unable to identify what has *actually occurred*. When there is no doubt that *some* of what we found is clearly the truth, we should distinguish it from what we *believe occurred*. There is a military term used to distinguish between what actually occurred and *beliefs*. What actually occurred is called *ground truth*, a term we hear on the news in time of war.

Although the term "ground truth" is used primarily by the military, it is also used by NASA, and by people who work in the hard sciences. In the military, *ground truth* is used to denote actual positions, such as where enemy tanks and troops are located. By definition, ground truth is *the actual state or true position of things at a given time.*

Ground truth is also used in the government's intelligence community to measure the accuracy of intelligence. When we go to war, we want our soldiers to be in the best possible position to defeat an enemy. When a U.S. intelligence officer presents information on the state of an enemy's situation - for example, how many troops or tanks are in a given spot - this information can be used to develop a plan to defeat that enemy. The quality of information presented in intelligence reports is measured relative to ground truth, which may not be available until later. The military works to obtain the highest quality of intelligence to improve its perceptions of the actual state of affairs.

To illustrate these concepts, Figure 2-1 shows an ellipse divided into sections. The center section is *ground truth*. Ground truth holds the actual shape of three objects. The outside sections show how these objects are perceived by Person A and Person B. Although some of these perceptions are similar to the actual object, they are all distortions of ground truth.

Survival of the Human Race

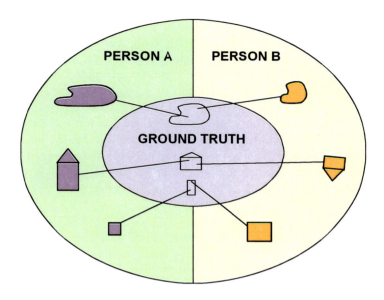

Figure 2-1 Perceptions of the true shape of objects by two different people.

These objects can be used to represent events and their interpretations as they may occur in real life. There are many reasons why people may have distortions of the truth; for example, not having enough time to view an event or occurrence, or not being able to view it well. Studies have shown that the human brain remembers what it thinks is important to remember[1]. This form of filtering is based upon our training. Although it may be unintentional, this filtering causes a bias in what we perceive really happened. As a result, people can end up with great differences in their perceptions of past events, especially when emotional factors prevail.

Engineering surveyors can put a pipe in the ground and identify its precise location within an inch. If other pipes are placed within 50 yards, and their distances from the reference pipe are measured using high precision instruments, these measured distances will be very accurate. Such measures are called ground truth.

Survival of the Human Race 15

If two people are asked to estimate these distances independently, just by standing back and looking at them, their estimates will likely vary by a factor of ten or more from the engineering surveys. Although some of these estimates may come close to the measured values, they will generally be distortions of ground truth.

The distances in this example may be used to represent events and interpretations that occur during the course of our life that are important to us. In these cases, one must be on guard to uncover distortions of the truth. One must take enough time to gather the real information on an event or occurrence, or work to view it using tools that yield an accurate account of the truth.

If we are responsible for making critical decisions, we must try to get the best possible estimate of "ground truth" to make sure our judgments are based upon accurate information. Without accurate information, different people will likely end up with great differences in their perceptions of these events, especially when emotional factors prevail. When making critical decisions, emotions will impair their judgment.

It is often difficult to accurately pinpoint ground truth. Good intelligence officers are trained to seek information, analyze the data, and produce accurate estimates of ground truth. They are taught techniques to remove biases that typically occur, and to take into account distortions in observations and analysis. They learn about intelligence sources and how to characterize these based upon the quality of prior reports compared to subsequent verification of facts.

High quality sources of information are valuable, particularly when lives are at stake. British Intelligence has always been known for the high quality of its intelligence sources. This is spoofed in the popular James Bond - 007 movies.

Survival of the Human Race

Telling the Truth

Having accurately observed ground truth, one may still refrain from relating the true picture to another person, typically because it may not be in one's best interest. In fact, one may avoid getting into a situation where the truth must be disclosed. This is not an observation or perception problem, but a deception problem. *Deception* means that *one does not desire to be truthful*. If a person has problems with *telling the truth*, then they are apt to be deceptive.

Deception is a common practice in military tactics. The military tries to deceive the enemy into thinking things are different from the way they really are. It is seen as acceptable to be deceitful when someone is dealing with an enemy. In fact, the military has devised many approaches in distinguishing between "friend" or "foe," so that they know who they must deceive versus who they must be honest with. We are obliged to be truthful to our friends, but we are often best off deceiving our foe.

Sometimes people are in a position where telling the truth may hurt someone, such as a friend. In this case, one must balance truth with *consideration* for a friend's best interest. This is a very delicate balance. If one chooses to be deceitful, then they will have fear that the other person will find out. As President of the Czech Republic, Vaclav Havel said, "...Truth liberates man from fear." If you have truth on your side, you have less to worry about. There isn't any deceit to be uncovered that would turn your friends against you because you were dishonest with them, and they could no longer trust you. So, in any situation, one should not deceive friends. It is generally better to be brutally honest than to deceive. As proclaimed by Arthur Schlesinger, this is especially true when writing history[2].

Experience shows that, given enough time, the truth is generally exposed. When this happens, it is best to have truth on your side, especially if you are in a position of leadership.

There are cases where, instead of being deliberately deceptive, people may just give short shrift to carefully stating the facts. Biases may lead them to state what they would like others to believe is true, rather than declining to answer and admitting they do not know the real truth. Harold Geneen defined the term "unshakable facts" to cover this situation. In his book, *Managing,* he describes them as facts that are obtained by doing extensive research to be positively sure that what you have in the end is a "real fact," not an "unfactual fact."[3] He also states that the truth about facts "is that the so-called 'facts' are almost always colored by the bias of the man presenting them."[4]

This agrees with our point that facts may be shaded by biases. The only way to make sure you have true facts is to have the "unshakable facts." To get these, a person must work to obtain as much information as possible about the "facts" and to draw a logical, unbiased conclusion from the information at hand. Then to maintain good trust relationships with friends, one must tell the truth, the whole truth, and nothing but the truth.

Defining Integrity

An important complement to seeking and telling the truth is integrity. Integrity goes beyond honesty, or simply telling the truth. It is the careful balance of consideration and truth. While explaining the truth with integrity, one has to work to ensure that the person they are talking with obtains a full view of their perceptions, in other words the *whole picture* or *whole truth*. A person with integrity goes the extra mile to *make sure other people understand the situation completely*. A person with integrity will always have the other person's best interests in mind.

Survival of the Human Race

Integrity is essential in the military. A military person is expected to be absolutely honest and free of deception with a compatriot. A person with high integrity will go further in understanding the information that their friends are in need of, and provide any information that is helpful in satisfying that need. This goes beyond simply telling the truth. This ensures that those who need the complete true picture, to make the best decisions, will get that picture *without asking*.

People with integrity will have the desire to seek the truth, make sure it is passed on without question, and use this principle in every aspect of their life. When people seek the truth, they must get the "unshakable" facts, i.e. as close to ground truth as possible, and discard any misleading or deceiving information. Conversely, when people tell the truth they must do so with integrity to make sure they are sharing the whole truth.

* * *

While considering truth in general, a person must have the desire to seek it, tell it, and apply it in every aspect of their life. When people seek the truth, they must get the "unshakable" facts, i.e. as close to ground truth as possible, and discard any misleading or deceiving information. Conversely, when people tell the truth they must do so with integrity to make sure they are sharing the whole truth. Without truth, we live in a world of biased, distorted, and just plain incorrect perceptions. Does this sound like a productive environment, a place where you would like to live? Does this promote survival? It is our view that societies that promote integrity have the best chance for survival.

Survival of the Human Race

Survival of the Human Race

Chapter 3: Consideration

There are two Golden Rules.
One says *"Do unto others as you*
would have them do unto you."
The other says
"He who has the gold rules!"

The importance of consideration of others goes back in time, at least to the days of Christ. One does not have to be religious to recognize the basic idea. We know of no better way to describe it than that quoted by the Golden Rule *"Do unto others as you would have them do unto you."* It is important that we interpret "others" to mean "all others." We do not distinguish between humans of different race, nationality, or faith. Since we are concerned with survival of the human race, we simply interpret the Golden Rule to apply to the entire human race.

In this context, consideration of others provides a balance of truth with justice. One may easily argue that a person deserves a certain punishment based upon some truth. But that punishment must be balanced against all considerations affecting that person's actions. Without consideration, justice may be unfair. Examples of this are extensive, e.g., in the case of racial biases. With different measures for different people, how does one know right from wrong.

Survival of the Human Race

Truth Breeds Friendships

Based upon news reports, manufacturers of guns and ammunition appear to be doing a land office business these days. This is not due to an increase in the number of game hunters. One news commentator visited sporting goods stores to interview women who were buying guns for the first time - for protection. Sales of guns are up because of the increase in violence around the world. Just reading, listening, or watching the news media, it appears that the number of nations and other groups of people fighting and killing each other is at an all-time high. It is hard to watch an international news show without seeing pictures of armed men engaged in serious combat.

One has to wonder - How long do we have before someone pulls the *nuclear* trigger, starting the cascade to end it all? The possibility of such an Armageddon is described in the book, The Sampson Option, by Hirsh[1]. Remember the Bible story about Sampson? According to scripture, Samson's calling was to begin the deliverance of Israel from the Philistines. For this, he was given great strength - in his hair - which he kept a secret, until his lust for the beautiful Delilah. After revealing his secret to her, his hair was cut and he was imprisoned by the Philistines. During a ritual celebration in the Philistine Temple in Gaza, Sampson was brought out to be shown to the people. However, his hair had grown back and he was able to push over the main pillars of the temple, bringing it down on everyone, including himself. Hirsh's book is as revealing as the title is appropriate.

Violence and death are part of the daily struggle for survival among many animal species. But at the higher cultural level of humans, one expects civility. Even in the United States there are dangerous neighborhoods as well as safe neighborhoods. The difference is highly correlated with housing prices and income levels. Yet there are major disagreements among people in the "highest culture" groups about going to war. One only has to listen to our Congressional representatives and other officials at the highest levels in Government to witness it.

Survival of the Human Race

Why is this so? In some cases it is because of strong ethnic biases. But in most cases it is because of different perceptions of fairness and justice. Often, these differences are biased. When one seeks the underlying causes, they are typically driven by greed. When people act on their greed, they tend to generate hatred. This leads to differences as simple as the perception of "Who started the fight?" If this sounds juvenile, it is because of a very basic problem in the way we humans have been taught to think. Very few of us have been carefully schooled in the basic principles of truth, observation, and perception.

This has nothing to do with one's educational level. There are PhDs in Washington think tanks who make it clear by the papers they write that they do not understand these basic principles. Consider the following example:

> "I've always believed that 'truth' and 'facts' are nebulous things. Each of us has our own version of truth and reality, and it really comes down to beliefs. What do you believe to be real?"

Fortunately, the world has a community of scientists who understand the difference between beliefs and truth. Yet, not all people engaged in "supposed" scientific endeavors belong to this community. For example, some so-called "sciences" contain a significant membership that does not understand the definitions and principles of experimentally based science - sometimes called *hard science*. The hard science approach to truth - versus belief - is covered in Chapter 8.

If we seek the truth and tell it with integrity, we will build trust among our friends. In fact, building trust is what creates good friendships. If two parties want to form a friendship, they must build a trust relationship. This takes integrity on both sides. If one of the parties has conflicting interests, then they will likely encounter situations where it is not in their best interest to disclose the truth. This could lead to deception that, in turn, creates enemies. To maintain a friendship, we must be considerate. And this implies that we should be open and honest with our friends about any potential conflicts of interest.

Survival of the Human Race

Truth & Consideration Breeds Happiness

We have been talking about how truth can aid in our survival - as a person, as a community, as a nation, and as the human race. One of the ways this can come about is to work together to seek the truth. Let's consider an example in sports of how truth and consideration breeds happiness among opposing fans.

Joe Paterno, coach of the Penn State football team, is certainly the longest, if not the most famous, football coach of all time. On the field, he was well known for his tirades against referees who made calls that were not in his team's favor. When sitting in the huge Penn State stadium and hearing both sides yell about calls, one was concerned that tempers may get out of hand, something not traditional at that school.

So it was Joe himself who led the effort to have the National Collegiate Athletic Association (NCAA) use taped replays to review close calls. Now, either team can challenge a call at the risk of losing a time-out if the challenge is not upheld. Often to Joe's chagrin, the review does not go in his favor. But he no longer questions a call after the reviews. And the fans are satisfied also. Finally it makes it much easier for the referees. All they do is take more time to look at the replay - sometimes over and over from different angles - to make a call that people cannot argue with. The replay makes it easier for the referees to be *fair*. And this breeds agreement, even with one's foe.

The important point here is that the fans - on both sides - have been more considerate of each other. They are now satisfied - and much happier - with the calls. The replay facility provides a huge leap to ensure fairness. This is obvious when one sits in the stands in a very tight and important game. When people think the call is fair, they are willing to accept the outcome without a complaint, even when it goes badly against them. This is because it is considered a *fair* call.

Survival of the Human Race

What makes it fair? People trust that the referees are *telling the truth*. This is because the replay system provides a mechanism for the referees to go back and *seek the truth*, with multiple people watching carefully. So let's consider some obvious logical facts. In order to tell the truth, one has to know what the truth is, i.e., one must have found it. This implies that one has to first seek the truth. This, in turn, implies that there is a truth - and it is best if we work hard to seek it.

When enough people are seeking the truth because it is very important to them, they can get quite upset if they think they have been deceived in any way, particularly if the outcome is not in their favor. When these same people believe that they have been told the whole truth, and that the other parties are considerate of their welfare, they are much happier, independent of the outcome.

Making Fair Judgments

In a fair environment, judging right from wrong has nothing to do with wealth, nationality, religion or political affiliation. It depends only upon the actions of the person or team being judged. It is their *behavior*, and the results of that behavior, that count. Good competitors will want to determine where they stand with respect to the rest. In a fair environment, those who are the best will be judged the winners. As a result, fair environments will attract the best competition. The best competitors will focus on what it takes to win, and as a result, competition will increase and drive performance to higher levels. In sports, this has brought about the instant replay - to ensure fairness of judgment.

In a biased environment, judgments will be made that favor other factors, such as personal connections, financial contributions, etc. When winners are selected based upon friendships, group affiliations, or money, it will likely favor those that are not the best. Those who are the best will try to understand how decisions were made. When real competitors detect unfair judgments, they become discouraged, and will likely drop out - looking for a fair environment. The end result is that an unfair environment is not truly competitive.

Survival of the Human Race

Unfair environments will not foster the level of achievement reached in fair competition. Resulting performance will not be as high, and winners will not be prepared to compete against the best. Those viewing a competition are deceived if they are not on the inside, and have no knowledge of the unfair judgments being made. Instead, the biased environment fosters deception while lowering achievement.

In the political arena, there are no referees. In a democratic society, the voters only know what they see and hear through the media. The media requires broadcast licenses from the government, as well as financial backing. Getting favors from elected officials is as old as government itself. To get elected, representatives running for office must have the backing, if not a fair presentation of their views from the media. This becomes a careful balance of fairness versus conflict of interest. The longer politicians are in office, the more influence they have over those who control media licenses. It is not unusual for large political contributions to be provided with the expectation of friendly legislation. So what is the media equivalent of the replay in sports?

Rating the media based upon number of listeners or viewers is like ranking a team based upon the number of fans. It appears that we should consider a rating system that measures the media based upon accuracy of reporting, when the truth finally comes out. This implies an organization with the ability to go back and obtain the truth about what really happened, who said what, and how decisions were made. Only then can they rank the media coverage fairly. It may take years to discover the truth, but it would help motivate people to seek it. If this improved the fairness of judgment by the media, it would lead to a more fair and competitive society.

* * *

Please consider the following thoughts:

The greatest vulnerability in the world is greed, for it breeds deception and hatred, turning friends into enemies.

The greatest freedom in the world is gained from truth and consideration, for they breed trust and create friendships.

Survival of the Human Race

Chapter 4: World population growth

"Seek the truth, and the truth shall set ye free."
Motto of the CIA

On October 12, 1999, various news services and major Internet providers announced the celebration of the birthday of the 6 billionth person. To call attention to the problem of expanding populations, UN demographers had chosen that day to mark the point when the world's population would hit 6 billion. On that day the UN Secretary-General, Kofi Annan, visited Sarajevo. The city was chosen symbolically as the birthplace of Baby Six Billion. An estimated 370,000 infants were born that day. Five years prior to that, an estimate showed that the earth's population would reach the 6,000,000,000 mark in the year 2000, see Figure 4-1.

To this day, the estimate shown in the chart remains unchanged. The earth as a planet is effectively "shrinking" due to an extremely fast rise in population growth. This shrinking effect is amplified by dramatic improvements in technology, particularly in the fields of communication and transportation. This causes many societies to live closer together, becoming more interrelated. Major changes in one society can immediately cause tremors in another society.

Survival of the Human Race

We would like to believe that the estimate for the year 2027, the point where the population reaches 10,000,000,000, is highly overestimated. However, based upon our sources, Figure 4-1 remains the best estimate. It does not take much reasoning to see that we are clearly in the midst of an explosion of the earth's population.

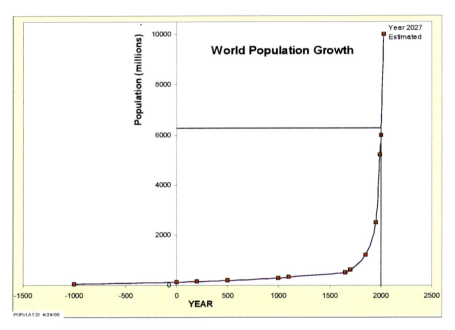

Figure 4-1. The exploding growth of the earth's population
(The data points shown were compiled using a number of statistical sources).[1,2]

The human race is rapidly becoming a tightly interrelated set of vastly different societies, many of whom are dependent upon the survival of others. For the human race to survive beyond some distant point in time, at least one of these societies must survive beyond that time. What will it take to ensure our survival further and further into the future? The question that needs to be addressed here is: What must a society do to maximize its likelihood of survival as far into the future as possible?

Survival of the Human Race 28

This book's purpose is to create a basis for maximizing our chances of survival. Creating such a basis requires establishing principles and definitions that are based upon solid (unshakable) facts, or derived from such facts using reason that is logically consistent. This alone is not as difficult as it may sound. The difficulty is not the ability to discover facts. Nor is it to use them to deduce additional facts. The real difficulty lies with the resistance to seek the truth.

People can agree with the need to ensure survival. But when it comes to discovering what it will take - seeking the truth - the defenses go up very fast.

Why does this occur? Because seeking the truth involves starting with a clean slate. And this implies wiping out existing beliefs that many people cling to - not for survival, but for hope. There have been books written on this issue. One of them, in the field of business management, is entitled "Hope is not a strategy!" This is more easily accepted in a business environment. But what happens in a political environment, when many people are very happy with the status quo, and do not want to see change?

Politicians who have been in office for many terms are known to fight against change. Having seniority helps them to raise more money for the next election. And if they have been in office for a few terms, they know what the constituents that elected them want to see unchanged. This does not imply that everything is fixed. It does imply that things are moving in the direction that they like. It is easy to verify that most of the members of the U.S. Congress, both in the House and the Senate, have been in office for many terms. Change only occurs when the voters are hit hard - directly, as in the economic crisis of 2008.

Looking back at the curve of population growth, and knowing the political ramifications of addressing this very unpopular issue, it is likely to be ignored until it is clear there is not enough food and other resources to go around. But, by then, it may be too late.

Survival of the Human Race

The story of Easter Island is not the only one of its kind. Similar problems have occurred in the 20th century. Having visited China many times, it is instructive to understand the recent history of that huge nation. At one point, the population was growing beyond the ability to preserve the farmlands, let alone the forests, particularly where the dense population areas were concentrated - in the eastern region.

Having gone through a severe famine, the Chinese leadership had to make some very difficult decisions. Fortunately, enough of the leaders decided to seek the truth. Looking at the existing infrastructure, distribution systems, travel times, distances, and population densities, it was clear that the leadership made the correct decisions to face the severe changes that had to be made to avoid major catastrophes.

One of these decisions was the requirement to limit the migration of people into the cities. This was particularly important with regard to young people who were very mobile, better educated, and much more capable of contributing to the welfare of the people that they wanted to leave behind. This led to limiting the migration of young people into the cities, with good reason.

Another major decision was to limit the growth of the population. This was done by encouraging birth control, and taxing families based upon the number of children they had. Families were limited to one female baby. So if the first baby was a female, that was it. If the first was a boy, then another was allowed. This has resulted in a lopsided population, with an obvious shortage of females. Males have to compete hard for a female mate.

It is difficult to see similar political decisions being faced by politicians in many Western nations. It is most difficult to see such limitations being imposed in the U.S. However, as the world's population grows, such decisions will be made, either by sufficient numbers of people seeking and acknowledging the truth, or by catastrophic events that reduce the population by calamitous forces.

Survival of the Human Race

If the population problem is not addressed, then there will be inevitable warfare for scarce resources. As an example, it is hard to deny that this scarcity is already occurring with regard to the demand for oil. When a population continues to grow, demands will continue to increase with that growth. It is clear from the curve in Figure 4-1 that, in the case of oil alone, we will likely be in a severe fight for its availability before 2020. We encourage the study of demand for the necessities of life: food, clothing, and shelter, so we understand what the limitations of our planet really are. Energy is but one scarce commodity that is starting to prevail on the civility of our nations.

* * *

We believe the survivors will be those who have the fortitude to both seek and expose the truth. They will be the ones who gain the knowledge of how to survive and have the courage to use it. As history has shown, only those people will be prepared to make the hard decisions, exert the energy to change direction, and invoke the self-discipline to improve their likelihood of survival.

Survival of the Human Race

Survival of the Human Race

Chapter 5: Allegiance

" I pledge allegiance to the flag
of the United States of America,
and to the Republic for which it stands,
one Nation under God, indivisible,
with liberty and justice for all."

Every U.S. citizen knows the *Pledge of Allegiance*. When we were in school, we saluted the flag at assemblies and at sports events. "In saying the Pledge of Allegiance, Americans 'pledge,' or promise, their 'allegiance,' or loyalty, to the flag. By being loyal to the flag, we are implying loyalty to our country, what America stands for, and those who sacrificed their lives so that we could be free."[1]

The Pledge of Allegiance is a powerful personal commitment. It is significant in terms of what is being pledged to our country and what is meant by it. So what is *allegiance*? And what role does it play in our everyday life?

Survival of the Human Race

Defining Allegiance

Besides its use in the Pledge of Allegiance, what does the term allegiance mean literally? The dictionary definition of *allegiance* is *the act of loyalty or devotion, as to a cause, person, government, country, etc.: or the act of binding oneself (intellectually or emotionally) to a course of action.* A person may have allegiance towards one's family, friends, teammates, coworkers, etc. The level of allegiance a person holds towards these things defines their pledge to act with sincerity.

When a person promises allegiance towards friends, it implies that those friends can expect that person to act with integrity and consideration towards them. By their acceptance, they should act the same towards the person making the pledge; else, they should be honest about *not* being able to keep such a strong commitment. By ensuring integrity and consideration in our friendships, we will increase our chance of survival. If everyone strived to follow these principles in relationships, then it would be prevalent in our communities and nations. All people should strive to act with integrity and consideration in every aspect of their life.

Conflicts Of Interest

Conflicting interests are a natural occurrence within as well as among societies. Not everyone wants the same thing. Everybody has individual goals and needs in their life, and sometimes these conflict with other people's goals and interests.

What we must keep in mind is that people will still have their own personal likes/dislikes, interests, and dreams. By being considerate and ensuring respect for each other's differences, we can maintain integrity and allegiance in relationships. If we do this, we should be able to overcome conflicts of interest through compromises that are fair to all sides.

Governments are always dealing with conflicts of interest. If everyone agreed on the courses of action to be taken by their government, there would be no need for political parties. The U.S. government revolves around our political parties and their interests for the nation. Each political party has distinct interests, so when they come together, there are conflicts. Such conflicts also exist within a party. In general, these conflicts lead to lobbying and other efforts to influence policy and spending.

But sometimes the conflicts become more complicated, involving multiple nations. For example, the idea of dual citizenship represents a major cause for conflicts of interest. No two nations are without conflicting laws and standards. So how is it possible to have allegiance towards two countries at the same time? If one is supposed to be fully loyal and devoted to one nation, how can that person be fully loyal and devoted to another nation?

There are various reasons why people obtain dual citizenships. Typical reasons are marriage with a person from a different country, and getting a job within a different country. But is it a good idea to let this happen in terms of U.S. national security? As Theodore Roosevelt stated, "We can have no 'fifty-fifty allegiance in this country. Either a man is an American and nothing else, or he is not an American at all."[2]

Dual citizenships clearly give rise to conflicts of interest when two nations have any disagreement or conflict with each other. How then can we be sure that someone will not use their citizenship in this country to help another country - where they may have a stronger allegiance on the issues? This leads to distrust at best, and more likely deception. We think Teddy Roosevelt had it right.

Survival of the Human Race

Treason

Treason is a very powerful word. People and governments take this term very seriously. Committing treason is a crime, one that must be paid for heavily. So, when we talk about treason, what do we mean? The definition of treason is the *betrayal of trust or faith; violation of the allegiance owed to one's sovereign or state; betrayal of one's country.* If we want a strong, secure nation, we certainly must not allow anyone to commit treason against it.

As stated earlier, we must practice integrity as citizens in our communities and nations, in order to achieve long-term survival. To ensure loyal citizens, one has to think long and hard about the idea of dual-citizenship and the potential for treason. But we don't think this is the only concern when trying to secure our nation's survival. We also have to look within. With this in mind, we must distinguish between friend or foe.

Friend Or Foe

What do we mean when we say *"distinguish between friend or foe"*? Walter Winchell once said, "A real friend is the one who walks in when the rest of the world walks out." Well, when we say "friend," we are talking about those people with whom we have allegiance and whom we can trust. When we say "foe," we are talking about those people who are not our friends but our enemies, those whom we would consider to be disloyal, and likely to be dishonest with us. The better we are at identifying and distinguishing between these people, the closer we come to achieving survival.

Survival of the Human Race

Nations are constantly gathering intelligence on each other to distinguish where they stand with respect to being a friend or foe. During times of conflict and war, we must know who to watch and be careful with, particularly when our security is threatened. Even in times of peace, it is extremely important to know who are your friends and who are your enemies. Knowing this will help us survive in a world that has many conflicts of interest.

Conflicts of Interest - Cause and Effect

How do conflicts of interest occur? They occur when friendships are compromised because a person who is supposedly a friend uses that friendship to accomplish an objective that is in conflict with the interests of their friend. If this occurs, their friend is deceived. The person with the conflict of interest is being dishonest and clearly lacks integrity. A real friend would declare that a conflict of interest exists, and would not make unfair use of the friendship.

When dealing with people with whom we have a strong allegiance we ensure that, even though we may have conflicting interests, these people will respect and understand our differences. We will be able to come to an understanding or a compromise easily and in a friendly, civil manner. But this is not the case when it comes to our enemies. This is obvious to see when we engage in war. Hopefully, we only go to war with countries that have declared us as their enemy, and with whom we cannot resolve our differences on any reasonable grounds. If these countries honestly wanted to be our friends, then there would be no need for war. We would solve these differences the same way we would with a friend.

This is not as easy as it sounds when dealing with powerful nations made up of people with strong distinct personal interests that may conflict within that nation. One year a nation may have many friends among other nations and the next have very few. This happened to the U.S. at the turn of the new millennium, when many of its allies had difficulty supporting a policy of preemptive strike.

Survival of the Human Race
37

In determining friendships among such nations, what is happening at the time, and the individual interests held within each nation become the deciding factors. When nations have similar interests, they will most likely become friends. But, if they have conflicting interests, then they are apt to become enemies. We must keep in mind that the positions of some nations, and their selection of friends, can change in relatively short time periods as the people who influence the politics change.

War between nations is often a one-sided desire, typically arising from greed that leads to hidden agendas and conflicts of interest. This leads to attempts to resolve conflicts that are deceptive if not clearly unfair. This situation arises because of the desire of sufficiently powerful people within one nation to take unfair advantage of the people in the other. When this occurs, the nation that is being unfair will resist or delay attempts by the other to resolve what may be contrived conflicts. It is often said that delay - in this context - is the worst form of deception.

***

As we strive to gain "real" allegiance with people in our lives, we build a foundation that supports us in our everyday life. If we are honest and act with integrity, we can expect to receive honesty and allegiance in return. If we are considerate with our friends, and follow the real golden rule, we can expect the same in return. We must look to develop relationships with those whom we can trust and whose allegiance will remain steadfast. We should avoid close relationships with those who may have conflicts of interest and would take advantage of our friendship. These guidelines will aid in our survival because we face less chance of betrayal. These individual values and principles should be applied to all aspects of our lives (family, community, politics, work, etc.).

Survival of the Human Race

Chapter 6: History

"History is the devil's scripture."
-Lord Byron

What is history? What goes into recording it in written texts? How are we sure that what is written down is what actually occurred? We all make the assumption that history is factual. But how can we be sure this is the case? How do we know? Where is the proof? Historians, who may have their own opinions and biases about events that have occurred, write our history. They have their own *perceptions* of what occurred. Is what they perceived what actually occurred? Can we trust them to be objective when preserving our history?

These questions and many more must be raised in order to be sure that our history is written down with the "unshakable facts." We must make sure that history is represented with the utmost objectivity to ensure it represents a true record of the past. We need the truth in all aspects of our lives, particularly our past.

Survival of the Human Race 39

Defining History

We will begin with a broad definition of history. *History* is not only a subject that we learn in school, but *a way of describing events that have happened in the past.* It purports to describe where we came from, and how we got here. It is supposed to help us to discover all the events, causes, effects, and obstacles that the human race has survived to get to where we are today. It professes to help us learn to avoid the bad outcomes created by past mistakes and aid in our survival.

However, people can use history as a weapon. Arthur Schlesinger, Jr. discusses this in his book *The Disuniting of America*. He states, "As the means of defining national identity, history becomes a means of shaping history. The writing of history then turns from a [concept] into a weapon."[1] Using history as a weapon can become very dangerous in terms of our ideas and views of the past. It becomes dangerous because these views and ideas become misperceptions if they have been altered in any way. If this is the case, how can we *learn* from the past? *How can we make good decisions today based on what happened yesterday, if our view of the events of yesterday is not what took place?*

Preservation Of History

How do we go about preserving history, accurately depicting the truth about what occurred? Historians supposedly take events as they occur and write them down. In his book *1984*, George Orwell's Party slogan was: "Who controls the past controls the future, who controls the present controls the past."[2] Historians have a great deal of power at their disposal. Is it possible that historians use history as a weapon? Do they distort it in any way? We may never know - unless we work hard to seek the truth.

Re-Writing History

Have you ever played the game of telephone? It begins with everyone standing in a line. The first person thinks of a sentence and whispers it in the person's ear next to them. Then that person whispers it to the person next to them. This continues down the line until it reaches the last person. Then the last person has to repeat what was whispered in their ear out loud. The reason this game is so amusing is because what comes out at the end is always completely different from what was originally said. People laugh at how distorted the sentence became through the "telephone line." If there are more than twenty people, one can ask every fifth person what they heard. In this way one can hear the evolution of multiple distortions. This is even funnier.

With the game of telephone, you always find out what the original message was; you learn the "truth." Most important, you learn how badly it became distorted each time it was retold. Yet when reading history, how do we know what the truth is? We take for granted that historians pass down the truth from century to century. As we learn from the telephone game example, what is retold generally gets distorted - with each retelling.

Have you ever considered that most historians must use "already written" history books to write new ones? If history is about the facts of what had taken place, then why would people want to rewrite them over and over again? The truth is, they *re-write* history. Every time a new history book is published, there has to be something different about it to stand out from the other ones; so, the history must be written differently - different events, different views of what happened, i.e., a different *history*. Ancient history has been re-written so many times that, by now, how do we know what really happened? We may know the basics, but when it comes to the details - the most important information - how much have they been altered? If this works like the game of telephone, it will be difficult to find out.

Survival of the Human Race

We must understand that there are several ways of distorting history. Some are unintentional like the game of telephone. Others seek to intentionally misrepresent the events that occurred. Either way history is misrepresented.

Misrepresenting History

When we read history books, we assume the presentations are accurate and unbiased. However, as we have discussed, this is not necessarily true. The result is that there are history books that are at odds with one another. This is particularly true when comparing the history about a particular nation - written by someone within that nation - to that written by someone in another nation. If we have to deal with historians contradicting one another, how do we find out what actually happened? How do we know what the truth is? Why would we want to find out in the first place?

We want to find out because, *to maximize the probability of survival, one must maximize the likelihood of making good decisions. Good decisions depend upon the information upon which the decisions are made.* This implies getting correct information. To get the correct information, one must seek the truth, understand it, and make maximum use of it. When history books are written to bias certain views, they are of little value when it comes to making good decisions based on cause and effect.

When historians decide what to record and how to record it, there isn't any specific process as to how this must be done. In most fields of research, science has defined a careful process for acceptance of *facts* to ensure that measurements are accurate, i.e., as close to reality as possible, with minimal error. However, authors of history books have much more leeway than authors of books in the "hard" sciences when it comes to stating the *facts*.

Survival of the Human Race   42

Misrepresenting the Present

Most people read newspaper and magazine articles, not history books. These articles are usually about recent events or issues. In such articles, the variation in perception is wide. This variation allows for opposition. We can pick up two different newspapers on any given day and get *opposite views* of "reality" regarding a certain subject or occurrence. This can happen for several different articles a day!

Along with articles, TV shows regularly host opposing views to expose different *opinions* about reality. One person says 'this' happened while the next person says 'that' happened. Newspapers and TV carry the most exposure of all media for passing information, and the variation in perceptions of reality is often very wide. Since great differences exist in perceptions of reality within one culture, the differences across multiple cultures are even more extreme. This is demonstrated on the Internet where anyone around the world can have a web site, or be a "blogger," and publish their views. The biases are clear. The real question is "What is the truth?"

To understand the potentially huge differences in perception of reality from culture to culture, we will consider a story written by Ruben Mettler, a former CEO of TRW.[3] The story is about his experience while on a guided tour of islands in the South Pacific shortly after World War II.

While touring one of the islands, Mettler visited an abandoned air base that had been used as a supply depot during the war. Mettler described what he witnessed as he got closer to the base. He could see natives wearing old tattered army uniforms, marching in formation up and down the old runway. He saw a man at the end of the runway holding a pair of carved wooden binoculars, pretending to look through them into the sky. In the old radio tower, he saw men talking into carved wooden radios, pretending to have conversations with people in the air, or at a distant site.

Mettler asked the guide what was happening. The guide responded that these men believed that, if they imitated what the Americans did during the war, they could get big planes to land and drop off booty, just as they did before.[4]

This story was published in Business Week magazine to demonstrate the absurdity of differences in perception. These South Sea island men thought that they were doing what was needed to bring down large aircraft from the sky to unload vast stores of food and supplies. They had no idea of the complexities involved to really make that happen. They all had good intentions, but their naiveté took them far astray from reality. Mettler concluded in the article that, "I am often struck by the similarities between our behavior and that of these primitives of the South Sea Islands. Both societies suffer from a failure to perceive reality or an unwillingness to act upon it. The difference is mainly one of degree. But any society that acts upon false perceptions of reality is in serious trouble."[5] Mettler was relating the natives' misperceptions to those being espoused by certain political leaders at the time (1980). Politicians consistently use events (sometimes referred to as *media* events) to advocate their own beliefs, often holding totally opposing views, implying that *at least one of them is false.*

As we try to gain an understanding of history, we must be aware that so many political leaders have a history of trying to impose *their perception of what is happening* on everyone, as they try to satisfy their own personal interests. To do so, they have become known for hiding, clouding, or even destroying any real evidence for true comparison.[6]

Given the above considerations, one must think about different cultures and the extent to which people go to "preserve" their cultural history - in the way they want it to be recorded. They may want to misrepresent the present, to place it in their favor - to preserve the perceptions they want to espouse. This, in turn, will misrepresent the true history. If this has been going on for centuries, how do the people from such a culture know what their true history really is?

Survival of the Human Race

History Repeating Itself

Have you ever heard the phrase 'History repeats itself'? Well, we now have a likely cause. We believe it is because of the way history was written. If people don't record the true history, then how can one learn from prior mistakes? If people are inhibited from learning about the real cause of past mistakes, they are prone to make the same mistake again. This is because the true cause of the mistake was not properly recorded. Thus, history repeats itself.

A society led by greed fosters deception. Problems incurred by such a society are typically blamed unfairly on others. When this occurs, the true cause of problems within such a society is hidden. The end result is that such a society cannot learn from its past mistakes.

We can now address the problem of determining the likelihood of survival for different societies over a long period of time. Given that societies come and go, various questions arise. How long will they survive? Can we determine which societies will last longer than others? Being able to answer these questions will require a true understanding of the past, as well as what is currently happening. This is assuming that we can uncover the true facts of the past, and have objective people stating the present. In general, if the history of events that brought harm to a particular society does repeat itself, then the likelihood of survival for that society will be less than one that learns from its mistakes.

To expand our understanding of which societies will last the longest, let's consider standards of living. Our measure of the relative standard of living of a society is simply as follows: *The society with the higher standard of living is the one that ensures the survival of its people for a longer period of time.* To learn why a particular society did not survive, we must have an accurate history. Without an accurate history, we are like the South Sea island natives.

Assuming we could trust sufficient historic evidence to be able to measure the relative standards of living in a number of societies, we then face a much larger problem: determining cause and effect. Understanding why one society has achieved a higher standard of living than another requires the ability to measure the accuracy of various competing cause and effect prediction models. We must be able to observe a sufficient number of experiments over sufficient time periods to witness differences in the ability to survive within societies.

But societies are not constant over time; they change. Their cultural approach at one time may be considerably different from that at another time. To perform such experiments on societies requires that they accept the technology and scientific approach required to obtain the precise information that describes cause and effect. Politically this may be very hard to achieve. Scientists must have access to accurate information about what is really happening, i.e., accurate perceptions of reality. Only then can they correctly record events for future use that will provide a sound basis for future experiments and prediction of future outcomes.

Even if the political hurdles can be overcome, accomplishing this for very complex societies is quite difficult. Dealing with these types of complexities is common in the field of engineering. Improvements are made in the design of bridges, skyscrapers, aircraft, etc., by experimenting and using prediction models. First, performance measures must be well understood. Then cause and effect relationships can then be modeled by design, and compared with reasonable accuracy because these structures remain constant over time.

As we attempt to record events that will lead us to an understanding of cause and effect, and develop prediction models that will validate our hypothesized relationships, we must dig deeper into our "perceptions" of reality. To do this implies seeking the truth, without prejudice as to what we may uncover. This involves understanding the measurement process and the fundamentals of the scientific method. More importantly, it requires that we are prepared to throw out prior beliefs if they do not hold up to the real test - of accurately recorded history.

Survival of the Human Race

This, we feel, is the hardest part - getting people to question their own deep beliefs. The most difficult task is getting people to seek honest answers when they are at odds with current practice. This is especially true when current practice is convenient, provides what is believed to be personal security, and may even be profitable. This is the common trade-off between short-term versus long-term benefits.

People may not think of the future survival of their society as being a long-term personal benefit. In fact, if the long-term survival of their society is at odds with their personal security, they may be faced with a major conflict. Unless their immediate society is directly threatened, and the deterioration of that society will personally affect them, people will usually defer to their own personal security. This does not preclude other motivations, such as heavy peer pressure, from affecting their decisions.

* * *

It is important to be able to see history for what it really is. If the historians and the news media of a society distort its history in any way, it will likely be detrimental to its people and to that society as a whole. It reduces their chance of survival. A society must know the facts about what goes on in its world to ensure that it will survive longer. In order to prolong survival, it needs to seek the truth when writing its history. It must demand the "unshakable facts," even if they "shake" current beliefs.

Only with the facts can one understand the true cause and effect relationships that resulted in negative outcomes. Otherwise, the same mistakes are made again and again, as history repeats itself.

Survival of the Human Race

Chapter 7: Measurement

"Two and two the mathematician continues to make four,
in spite of the whine of the amateur for three,
or the cry of the critic for five."
-James McNeill Whistler

When people think about measurement they usually think about measuring tools, such as rulers, measuring cups, stop watches, etc. These are the simplest tools for measurement. We use measurement in all aspects of our lives, when we cook, in sports, in music, when building houses, even when we plan out our day.

Measurement typically has a broad array of levels. When we looked up the word 'measure' in various dictionaries, the list of definitions abounded. Along with the standard use of the word measure, we also have many phrases that contain the word "measure," such as: to "measure up" and to "take measures." When we say 'one needs to take measures,' we are talking about taking some sort of action. So a measurement can also be an action that needs to take place in order to resolve an issue or gain information.

Survival of the Human Race   49

When we ask 'does one measure up' to something, we are comparing that person to something they are being measured against. In looking over the various definitions, the word measure is generally used to imply a comparison of one thing to another. But what exactly do *we* mean when we talk about measurement?

In order to fully understand the meaning of measurement, we start with a discussion about distributions. Only by understanding distributions, will we be able to bring the idea of measurement into better perspective.

Defining Distributions

So, what are distributions? Generally, a *distribution* is *the arrangement of a set of measures grouped according to some characteristic quality, such as frequency, time, or location.* Distributions can show you how many people in a given population hold a certain characteristic and where these characteristics lie throughout the breakdowns of a society in any given way, i.e. gender, nationality, wealth, etc.

Using a classic example, consider the breakdown of students according to scores on a given test. The resulting distribution is illustrated in Figure 5-1. The score brackets used are 0-5, 6-10, 11-15, etc., to a maximum of 96-100. These are labeled across the bottom axis of the chart. The number of students in a bracket is labeled along the left-hand axis of the chart. Various statistics can then be computed to characterize the distribution. For example, only 1 student received a score lower than 40; 7 students received a score between 60 and 65; and only 1 student received a score over 95.

Survival of the Human Race

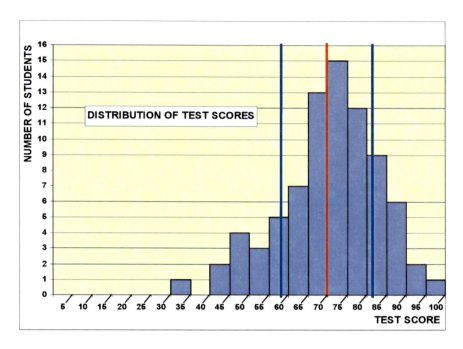

Figure 5-1. Example of a distribution.

The *mean* or *average* score occurs approximately at 70 as shown by the red line. By mean or average we imply that the total area in the bars on the left of the red line equals the total area on the right. To compute the average, one multiplies the value of the measure in the middle of a bracket (test score) times the number of samples (people) in that bracket, and sums them over all brackets. Then one must divide this sum by the total number of samples (people) in the population being measured.

The *variance* is another statistic measuring the amount of variation from the mean. This is somewhat more complex to calculate. One can think of the variance measure as the average distance from the mean. This is shown by the blue lines in the figure. We now consider a basic definition - the law of distributions.

The *Law of Distributions* states that *every property of a population, individual, or element of nature is, in general, characterized by a distribution with a finite variance.* For example, all societies (cultures, nationalities, races, etc.) have properties whose distributions have relatively wide variances, just within their individual populations. Measures of height, weight, intelligence, strength, self-discipline, etc., will all vary widely within a given society. These measures can be tested experimentally.

Representing Distributions of Large Populations

Figure 5-2 represents a typical distribution of a large population. Unlike Figure 5-1, the number of performance brackets in Figure 5-2 is extremely large (each bracket is extremely small), so the distribution can be approximated by a smooth curve. On the right side of the curve lie those people who are in the higher performance brackets, while the people at the left are in the lower brackets. The mean (average) is shown as μ_a.

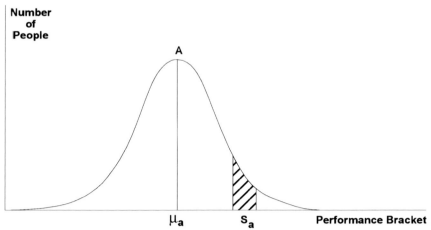

Figure 5-2. Example of a distribution of different people's performance.

A sample segment (S_a) of the population in Figure 5-2 is shown relative to the performance bracket spanned by that segment. All of the samples in that segment have similar performance measures.

One of the most important facts to observe when studying a group of people is that, by definition, 50% of the people are below average and 50% are above. This is independent of what is being measured. There is no way to change this. By definition, it is the inherent nature of a distribution - a mathematical fact!

When dealing with very large populations, characterizing every element (person) can be very time consuming and expensive. To simplify the measurement process, one may select samples - on a *random* basis - to characterize the population. By random, we imply *unbiased*. For example, if one wanted to determine how many people were over 6 feet tall in a population of 10 million people, one could pick 1000 people *randomly* to come up with a reasonably accurate answer. Determining how to sample a population is a significant scientific problem. One must ensure that the selected samples are truly random and that a sufficient number of samples is taken. This is done to ensure that the set of samples fairly represents the entire distribution of the population. We must stress that this is a simplified explanation.

As indicated above, distributions are used to compare the properties of different societies. We will compare two different societies below, and we will be able to see how one can use (and misuse) distributions to compare the differences.

Misrepresenting Distributions

Figure 5-3 illustrates the distributions of two different societies A and B. We note that the performance of these two societies overlap significantly. These overlapped areas may cause confusion in characterizing each population. For example, the means, variances, and other statistics are quite different, yet they are clouded by the overlap.

Survival of the Human Race

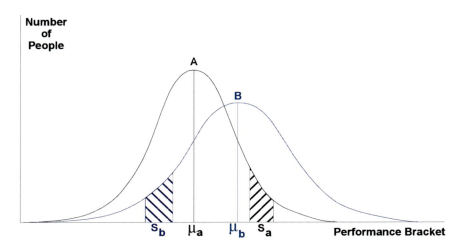

Figure 5-3. Overlap of different population distributions.

Even though the samplings of the two societies are quite different, they can be made to look similar. In fact, it is easy to depict them unfairly. As an example, one may observe a sample of people (S_a) in society-A who are in a higher performance bracket than a sample of people (S_b) in society-B.

If we use these sample sets to compare the people in the two societies, we conclude that the people in society-A are much better performers than those in society-B. Yet, when looking at the figure more closely it is not hard to see that the average performer in society-B performs better than the average performer in society-A by a reasonable margin. Using small (and biased) sample sets - such as S_a and S_b - to make the comparisons can do wonders to distort statistical measures.

The Need for Accurate Sampling

The Law of Distributions is ignored when people draw broad generalizations using single sample points or small sample sets that are biased. As an example, a person may say that all doctors are curt. This is a broad generalization based upon a small sample of doctors (maybe only one) that a person is familiar with. Since the typical person only knows just a few doctors, they are easily biased in their thinking, particularly when they assume that all doctors act the same way. Using a small set of biased samples, a person may draw almost any conclusion they want.

Since people in a given performance bracket may naturally tend to associate together, for example - live in the same town, samples taken in one area of a state may not be representative of those in another area of the same state. This provides the basis for drawing wrong conclusions based on samples that are not representative of the population. This is a well-known problem in statistical sampling.

When trying to characterize a particular distribution across a large population, it tends to be difficult to gain an accurate sampling. As stated earlier, this is a common problem in statistical sampling. Without a careful design of the sampling process, it is extremely difficult to draw a general conclusion about a given population, particularly if that population is spread out over a large area. In addition, when sampling people's viewpoints, one can encounter particularly wide variations.

In order to avoid the misrepresentation of distributions, one must ensure that the approach to statistical sampling of a population is accurate. This means that it will take a reasonable design and test process to ensure that a valid sampling approach is used to represent the population as a whole. Accurately representing populations brings us back to our initial discussion on measurement.

Characterizing Societies Using Measurement

At any instant in time, the likes and dislikes of a society will vary widely among its total population. For example, some people will work hard to achieve total privacy and independence, while others will gladly be a ward of the state in return for their security. Perceptions of morality and the importance of family life, education, and other properties of a society will vary widely. In fact, there are wide distributions across a large population in just about any area of comparison.

Given that we can quantify the distributions that represent pertinent measures of societies, we can use them to characterize selected traits of different societies. One can then design experiments to characterize specific features in a particular society or population, to obtain the distribution data they need. In our case, we want to measure the likelihood of survival.

We must also note that these distortions and their resulting measures will vary with time. People's likes and dislikes change. If we can observe these changes, we may see where things are heading.

$$* * *$$

Having a good understanding of the important distributions representing a society, and how they affect the future behavior of that society, a person will have the knowledge to see where a society may be heading compared to other societies. Accurately representing these distributions, and the manner in which they are changing with time, is critical when measuring the desired characteristics in a given society, and populations as a whole. When conclusions are drawn from biased and distorted measures, measures that paint a rosy picture of reality, a society is prone to poor judgment on the part of its leaders. When a society uses accurate measurement facilities to compare itself to other societies, that society moves closer toward the knowledge necessary to improve its chances of survival.

Survival of the Human Race

Chapter 8: Science

"I am sorry to say there is too much point to the wise crack that life is extinct on other planets because their scientists were more advanced than ours." - JFK

The actual practice of real science is not very familiar to most of us. Some percentage of high school students take biology, and maybe physics or chemistry. Even those that took these classes may ask - What do we actually use science for? How does it affect our lives?

Most of us think about science only when we hear things on the news, such as when there are space shots, new drugs or vaccines, new discoveries, new technologies, etc. Sometimes we hear political arguments about limiting the practice of science in certain areas. Beyond these brief encounters, most of us don't come into direct contact with the practice of hard science. But when we turn on the radio or TV, what happens? Where do the "radio waves" come from? When flying on planes, how do they work? When using cell phones we do not think about how calls are routed; we just press a button to call a friend. So whether we realize it or not, science is a very important part of our society and universe. We cannot - and should not - disregard it.

Survival of the Human Race

In fact, we should embrace science because it is another avenue down the road to getting to know ourselves, our society as a whole, and to ensure our survival. It will help us to understand more clearly why certain things are the way they are, and why events take place when they do. Understanding science will give us a better understanding of how the world really works and will bring us closer to being able to gain factual information about our environment.

Defining Science

What is science, and what are the concerns of people who use scientific methods? Generally speaking, *science is a discipline for observing and describing behavior in the physical world.* The scientific method is used to learn about cause and effect. But it requires experimentation in a careful and rational manner to learn how and why things happen.

Scientists begin asking questions like "how" and "why" to start understanding their issues. They are generally motivated to obtain knowledge to improve the future of the human race. Given that there may be some disagreement as to the means, the principal concern of *most scientists* is ensuring survival of the human race. (We note that there have been major disagreements among scientists working on the development of nuclear weapons. Einstein was in a small minority of people who were against it.) Ensuring survival is demonstrated by a quest for improvements in the way we live over the long term.

We believe that the expansion of scientific knowledge is an important factor for ensuring our long-term survival. This requires a cultural environment that is conducive to learning and appreciating scientific methods and facts. It also requires that a sufficient number of people become both *seekers and purveyors of truth.*

The Scientific Method

Science requires seeking the truth through the scientific method. The scientific method begins with experimentation, which provides the basis for establishing *scientific facts*. We must encourage experimentation, and the accurate reporting of experimental results, to obtain the truth. To do this, we must ensure precise measurement. This will lead to accurate perceptions of reality. We must guard against forces that inhibit such experimentation, for they will only serve to suppress the truth.

These concepts must be understood and appreciated by a sufficient number of people in a society in order to establish and maintain the freedom to seek and speak the truth. With this freedom comes a higher likelihood of survival.

The scientific method uses observation, deduction, and prediction in order to take measurement error into account. Unless the truth can be observed directly, statements about perceptions of reality must be qualified in terms of probabilities, and confidence in the probability statements. These statements must be derived from valid measures of distributions. They must be calculated in terms of probable error in measurement. The *Uncertainty Principle* from quantum physics tells us that *there is some finite likelihood of error in all measurement*, albeit in many cases, too close to zero to be concerned about. To develop an accurate assessment of a situation, one must get as close as possible to the facts about actual events that occurred. The ability to do this can be reached through the scientific method.

The more important a judgment or decision, the more important it becomes to ensure the accuracy of information used to make that decision. This is where the scientific method is important. In a military environment, knowledge of the enemy situation (military intelligence), and knowledge of how to counter the threat typically makes the difference between winning or losing battles.

Survival of the Human Race

Experienced military organizations place a high value on intelligence gathering, analysis, and interpretation to gain an accurate perspective of the enemy situation. In order to achieve this, one must use a scientific approach. By gathering *scientific facts* about the enemy, military intelligence attempts to gain the knowledge needed to counter the threat.

Scientific Facts

A *scientific fact* is *a statement about the behavior of a physical entity or phenomenon that can be confirmed by repeatable experiments.* The ability for independent organizations to repeat experiments and verify a theory describing observable behavior provides the foundation for scientific facts. Unless an independent party can repeat an experiment that verifies a theory, there is not sufficient evidence to support that theory. Unless verified in this manner, a theory is considered an unproven hypothesis from a scientific standpoint.

Einstein waited 15 years before his General Theory of Relativity was confirmed by an experiment that required an eclipse of the sun. Separate teams of scientists performed the experiment and confirmed the accuracy of his predicted results.

When we were discussing "unshakable facts" in Chapter 2 on truth, there had to be absolute proof to be sure we are talking about 'facts.' Once we have the facts, we are generally able to make good decisions.

It is a scientific fact that the earth is changing, and not just because of things that humans are contributing. It is changing whether or not we are here. In fact, it is changing in ways over which we have no foreseeable way to control. It is up to us to use these facts to gain an understanding of survival as it applies to the human race living on earth.

As scientific knowledge grows about the physical laws of nature, one can more accurately determine what has happened in the past, and more accurately predict what will happen in the future. It is now an accepted scientific fact that our universe is expanding, with its galaxies rapidly spreading apart.

Astronomers, geologists, biologists, and anthropologists have studied the evolution of the formation of the earth, other planets, solar systems, galaxies, and our universe, as well as the coming and passing of various living organisms and species. The facts are that life, as we have come to know it; i.e., that which has been recorded for the last ten thousand years, is but a small instant in time compared to the life of planet earth, let alone the universe in which we live. Furthermore, the space in which we live on earth is but a tiny speck in a vast universe that is dealt with everyday by thousands of scientists, who are constantly probing its depths.

The facts stated above are just a diminutive portion of the scientific facts available to us. There are many facts available to us; we just need to seek them out. Scientists are constantly working to find out more, not only about our universe, but also about our planet and people in general. There are numerous scientific studies taking place today in a vast variety of areas, including the fields of agriculture, energy, and health care. We expect these studies to yield scientific facts that will improve our chances of survival.

Scientific Models

Whenever we attempt to predict the outcome of a set of events, we may go through a conceptual sequence of scenarios, and evaluate their probable results mentally, producing a set of possible outcomes. As a simplistic example, when we cross a street, the possible scenarios are as follows: crossing the street without looking; looking both ways first; waiting for the light to change; or waiting for a car to pass. These possible scenarios produce a set of possible outcomes, such as making it safely across the street or getting hit by a car.

Survival of the Human Race   61

This mental exercise is a type of conceptual scientific model, which is used to assess a situation. As problems get more complex, and we introduce more scientific approaches, we may consider using a more formal scientific model on a computer.

The most significant advances in the last half-century would not have occurred without computer models. Putting a man on the moon would not have been possible without significant computer models and simulation efforts using these models. Almost every aspect of a space flight is analyzed, designed, and tested by building detailed computer models and running simulations.

Since the early days of the 1950's, advancement of computer technology itself has depended heavily upon the development of very detailed computer models used to predict operational performance and reliability in computers. These models are used to accurately predict performance in live operating environments.

Another area benefiting from the use of computers is the medical field. Many more breakthroughs are likely given that more powerful computer technology continues to develop.

Economists have been building computer models for years, with scarce, if not disputed, success. One of the reasons for their lack of predictive accuracy is the difficulty of getting good experimental evidence, i.e., data that is reliable. A second reason argues how economists can misinterpret, and in turn misrepresent, historic data. This is evident from the work of Jacques Rueff.[1] Experimental evidence must come from accurate measurements and correspondingly accurate historical accounts of that evidence.

A third reason for the lack of predictive capability of economic and social models is the lack of important details that reflect large changes in outcomes based on small changes in inputs, representing nonlinear mechanisms. These are difficult to describe in general and, in the past, are difficult to represent in computer based mathematical models.

Survival of the Human Race

The lack of success of social and economic modeling in the past is only a reflection of the need for improved approaches to very complex analysis and prediction. A more scientific approach - one tied to real world experimental evidence - is certainly necessary. To achieve this, an environment must exist that allows biases to be removed so that people are free to discover the truth.

In an environment where the truth about a particular subject may be socially unacceptable, one may be inhibited from the high incentives needed to extract the true facts. If the subject in question is related to human survival, then the knowledge needed to survive may be hidden to the extent that it never becomes useful information. Yet this information may be necessary for our own survival. In a real scientific environment, researchers are uninhibited from discovering the truth. That is what science is about. If our nation is to survive, our scientists must be encouraged to *seek the truth,* no matter how much it goes against our treasured beliefs or emotions.

* * *

For us to be able to make decisions that lead us down the road to improving our chances for survival, we must understand the ways of science. A scientific environment is one that encourages seekers of the truth to discover the real facts, no matter what they disclose. Using the scientific method to observe and describe behavior, we are seeking the truth in a way that will yield the "unshakable" facts. We are able to tell the truth using scientific models that will be required to show the whole truth. Through scientific methods, we gain scientific facts. Through scientific facts, we gain factual knowledge. It is this knowledge that gives the key to unlock the door that leads to higher probabilities of survival.

Survival of the Human Race

Chapter 9: Relationships

"One must care about a world one will not see."
-Bertrand Russell

We must be able to apply the concepts we have discussed in prior chapters to our own lives and relationships with other people. Consider the different kinds of relationships we have with others. We have family, loved ones, friends, co-workers, etc. How can we increase our chance of survival through these relationships?

People build relationships for various reasons. They may want other people in their lives for support, companionship, and security. Another reason is because two heads work better than one. We like to solve problems or make decisions with the help of others because it provides another viewpoint, bringing more information into the picture. Most significant accomplishments require teamwork. Historically, it has taken the intimate relationships between men and women to ensure the survival of the human race - through reproduction and the family environment.

As we build relationships, we must be able to "maintain" them to ensure their survival. We must be able to have good relationships with many people in order to ensure survival of a community. Different communities must communicate and maintain good relationships so that states and nations will survive. From there we have international relationships, which make up our world. If we develop and continue our relationships based on integrity and allegiance, then we can ensure their continuing existence. As we develop more good relationships, everyone's chance of survival increases.

Survival of the Human Race

Layers of Relationships

A strong foundation of trust takes a long time to build; but it takes only a single breach to tear it down. When a person breaches your trust, you are aware they may do it again. So if trust breaks down, it takes a long period of time to build it back up. Trust is very important when it comes to relationships with people to whom we are very close. The people who are generally closest to us are our families, loved ones, and best friends. They have been around us the longest and know us the best, so we usually find the most support and trust within these relationships.

Other relationships are those with acquaintances and friends that are not considered our "best friends." These people are those with whom we work or who we meet through others. They may come and go as our life changes.

The rest of our relationships include all the people who we interact with in our daily lives but do not know personally. These are the people we pass in the street and smile at, the people with whom we stand in an elevator, people who we don't really know, but who live with us in our community.

All of these relationships combine to make up a community. The relationships that make up that community should be trustworthy and honest relationships. Whether we are dealing with family or talking to a member of our community that we don't know, we must act with integrity. Without these qualities in our everyday interactions with people, we decrease our chance of survival.

Survival of the Human Race

Communities

We all belong to communities. What is a community, and what does it consist of? A *community* is *a group of people who live, work, or socialize together as a smaller unit within a larger one.* A typical community is made up of many relationship layers.

Consider all of the different types of communities that make up our nation. There are family communities, school communities, working communities, senior citizen communities, etc. Generally, people who have things in common form a community. Interactions among these people create the atmosphere for the community. People in communities must respect each other and be honest with each other to build a positive community environment. This is what makes communities healthy and more apt to survive.

Communities of people have come and gone for centuries. Why do some survive and some become extinct? Certainly external factors can cause a small community of people to become extinct, such as when they experience earthquakes, hurricanes, floods, droughts, etc. Fortunately today there is sufficient scientific data on enough areas where people can settle with reasonable safety. Scientific technologies can provide sufficient advance warning, making it unlikely for *natural* disasters to wipe out a community.

Natural disasters notwithstanding, there are towns and even small cities in recent times that have gone from thriving, healthy, well-educated communities to almost ghost towns in one or two decades. Most people are familiar with an example of such a community. It is not unusual that many of the people close to these communities do not understand how or why things went from good to bad. However, it does not take much investigative research to determine that the root causes for deterioration are most likely disagreements among the inhabitants regarding what constitutes a desirable living environment. Connecting these disagreements, about what constitutes a desirable environment, with the quest for survival is much more subtle.

Private Versus Public Ownership

One way that community relationships can break down is by eliminating private ownership, and converting private property to public ownership. If private ownership of land or property does not exist, then people are not concerned about taking care of the property. Since it is not theirs, it would be foolish to place a personal value upon it because anyone else can take it and use it. There is no need to compete for anything because everybody is declared to have equal rights to all property in the eyes of the community. If such an environment is truly fair, then everyone is your equal, and there is no way to improve your status. The result is there is no motivation to work hard or compete.

Unfortunately, there is less need for truth and consideration in such an environment because no one has anything to protect. Breakdowns occur in such a society because the values of truth, consideration, and competition are undermined. The result is that politicians can distribute "wealth" in accordance with their need to stay in power. They can then determine who is "more equal". In such an environment, the politicians determine who lives where and who gets what. It then becomes a game of who owes whom what political favors.

Freedom of Choice

In a private community where the people own the property, they are free to choose where and with whom they want to live, within the constraints of how each wants to dispose of their own property. People are also free to invest in improvements to their property and the material things they need to get through life on a day-to-day basis. They will want to protect their own property to keep it safe and protected from harm. They will also want a higher authority to help them to protect it. They will want that higher authority to be fair and honest when it comes to making judgments on the destruction or confiscation of property, and the rights to privacy.

When people have something to protect, they start to understand the need to be fair and considerate of others. They have the motivation to strive for a better life because they are free to achieve it. Respect grows - as does competition. Competition can thrive because people are free to improve themselves and their property.

Competition

In an entirely public community, people are constrained to their allocations. They are neither free nor motivated to improve their environment, and therefore not motivated to achieve an improved life. Unless they resort to hiding property and deceitful politics, they cannot improve their lives substantially. Their lives remain the same, if not deteriorating, compared to communities that are free and private, and improving. This comparison has been conducted time and time again, and the results are apparent throughout history.

The Soviet Union presents a excellent example. The Soviet government owned all property, and the "whole economy was rigged in such a way that people often found it unprofitable to work."[1] The pay did not equal the effort put in or the result of the work. As the Soviet workers' folk saying goes: "You pretend to pay us, and we pretend to work." This type of government causes not only a stagnant economy, but also a stagnant life for its people.[2]

Privacy Versus Security

In an environment where competition is constrained, performance will also be constrained. If people are not allowed to excel, or not rewarded for excellence, they will not be motivated to excel. This is illustrated in Figure 7-1 where population A is constrained in their performance, either by rules or motivational factors. Population B is unconstrained in performance and encouraged to excel. When people are held back or discouraged from excelling, they will not perform near their "best."

Survival of the Human Race

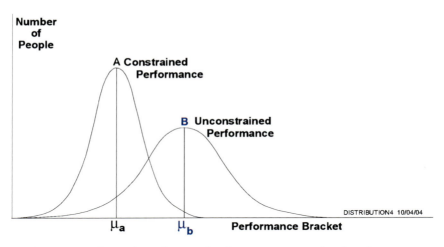

Figure 7-1. Illustration of constrained versus unconstrained performance.

Conversely, when people are rewarded for winning - being the "best," they work hard to excel. There are many examples of this phenomenon in controlled versus free market economies.

Another example of privacy versus security is jail. We can compare our private lives with those of the inmates. People who are in jail have no privacy. They live in barred cells, allowing easy inspection of their activities. Activities outside their cells are done collectively. They never have any privacy. But, there is one thing they do have, and that is security. They are very secure because everything they need to live, such as food, clothing, and shelter, is provided for them. They do not have to worry about money or property because they don't need these things.

On the other hand, people who live in a totally private environment are generally concerned about their own security. They can't be sure that they will always have enough money to have food, clothing, a bed, and basic needs. There is a trade-off between privacy and security. Some people have lots of both, but most people are generally concerned about one or the other.

As we concluded from the previous example, a community is more likely to survive if it provides privacy for its inhabitants. Security will be approached from a different perspective - to protect ownership and private property.

Community Decay

Another cause for the breakdown of a community is when its environment is changed. Positive environments are created by the ways of life of the people in that community. Once an environment begins to lack respect for privacy, the community may begin to decay. We must keep in mind that this change may happen gradually over many years. We must also understand the causes of decay and what a person can do to resist it. If people can resist decay in our communities, then their communities should survive much longer.

While a community is decaying, the community that is replacing it is growing. Because each community decays in a different way, people outside that community might not realize it is a decaying one. Keeping this in mind, consider the following example of the process of community decay.

The community we are going to discuss was considered desirable from a residential family standpoint. This community started out as a highly family oriented environment, where parents were concerned about providing a good place to raise their children. Children who grew up in this community strived to maintain this type of family environment. They appreciated what they gained from the community. It had an excellent school system. Discipline was enforced by parents who had worked hard to achieve what they had accomplished, and wanted to ensure their offspring had the same regard for discipline. The environment was very private, but at the same time the people were free to choose their own direction.

Survival of the Human Race

Town government was kept small, and people volunteered to help those in real need. Taxes were minimal, used only to provide for police protection, sanitation, zoning code enforcement, and schooling. These services were closely monitored by the residents.

As people in this community worked hard to constantly improve this type of environment, it thrived. The residents constantly developed and instilled a good sense of values, such as a very high regard for honesty (building trust) and a sincere consideration for their neighbors (building justice).

Most of the population had a very long-term outlook. Maximum time was spent building and improving the environment for future family life, and little time was spent trying to acquire riches quickly. Many people made money by providing for the town, not trying to take money away from it. Wealthy people outside this town who valued their own assets, and who wanted a disciplined lifestyle to protect them, began to desire homes there. The original inhabitants were then able to accumulate wealth in the form of long-term assets, as their properties became very valuable.

As this community became more and more attractive, as a place to visit as well as to live, it became apparent that commercial businesses that depended on shoppers from the outside were very valuable. This was because people who lived outside the town loved to go there and shop, to see how beautiful the town was, and to feel very comfortable walking about the streets. As time passed, it was clear that hotels, restaurants, nightclubs, and bars were particularly valuable because they could draw large crowds who wanted to visit and be associated with this town. Commercial interests knew they could make money by taking advantage of the town's very fine environment. Eventually this quiet family oriented town attracted a nightlife community. The family community started decaying, while the nightlife community started thriving.

Survival of the Human Race

The commercial interests were able to make political contributions, for which politicians in turn granted variances and licenses for hotels, bars, and entertainment facilities. The rest is history; unfortunately, it is the history of many towns.

There are two problems that usually occur when a town decays. One is that some of the politicians begin to shift their allegiance towards new benefactors. They begin to grant favors to commercial interests instead of protecting the interests of the community's residents. This leads to the second problem: a lack of integrity and allegiance that those politicians have towards the residential community versus their commercial benefactors, who typically live outside the community.

We must point out that measuring honesty of politicians also leads to a distribution. Many politicians are very honest. Unfortunately many are not, making it difficult for those that are. When dishonest politicians have a conflict of interest, they begin to act against the interests of the residents of the community. They lose concern for people's trust and become inconsiderate of their constituents.

Any community can be a healthy environment, as long as the people uphold their values. Those who increasingly dislike the community they are living in may choose to move elsewhere. Time and time again, history has shown that people leave their communities, and even their homelands, seeking to survive or improve their quality of life elsewhere.

Another issue is that different cultures desire different lifestyles. All people should be allowed to live the way they want, within their private communities, providing they don't impose their ideas on other communities. Everyone knows of a city with bars on every corner. It is easy to compare this type of life to that in villages with no bars. These are clearly different environments, serving their inhabitants with different purposes. Are one community's inhabitants more likely to be honest and considerate of each other than the other? Is one more likely to survive longer? This is where accurate history can tell us who has a better chance of survival.

Survival of the Human Race

The key issue here is that what is good for one group of people may not be considered good for another. Setting standards that are the same for everybody causes many problems, including the following:

- Individual freedom of choice is eliminated. People are not free to create or choose different environments. Politicians end up deciding what constitutes a good environment for everyone.

- Elimination of disparities inhibits real competition, eliminating the ability to achieve excellence.

- There is no way to measure the differences in possible outcomes because experimentation, and therefore observation of honest differences, is inhibited.

- It inhibits the ability to observe the true differences that result in the long run.

What is important is that whatever community we live in, we work to set the highest standards for integrity and expect our politicians to behave in the same manner, demonstrating their allegiance to those who have elected them. If we can achieve this, then our community has a good chance to survive.

To achieve these standards, we must work to spread the full understanding of truth and what is required to obtain it. We must also spread an understanding of the importance of consideration of one's fellow man. A community that values these two principles will help to ensure its political leaders do the same! We must also teach our children to behave with honesty and consideration towards others. If we achieve this in our communities, we believe that we have a chance to be a nation that will continue to survive for a very long time.

Survival of the Human Race

Nations

Our world is made up of many nations. As we discussed earlier, a nation is made up of many communities. We know what is needed to make up a great community, but how do we get to be a great nation?

The effort must begin within our communities. With enough communities having the survival properties described in the previous section, we can build a great nation. Just like communities, nations go through decay also. There have been many nations in our history that have come and gone, or replaced by new nations. If a nation's communities are replaced with new ones that practice high degrees of integrity and allegiance, then we believe the new nation has the ability to achieve a higher likelihood of survival.

* * *

Relationships begin with the individual. If individuals have a good sense of values with regard to truth, consideration, and allegiance, then they can pass these on to others through relationships. These values determine the make up of a community, and contribute to building a great nation that has a good chance of survival. Communities increase their chance to survive by electing officials who are trustworthy and considerate individuals. Communities need politicians who have allegiance to their constituents and look out for the peoples' interests, not their own personal gain. This implies that a community's constituents have also pledged their allegiance to that community, else they are betraying their neighbors that have trusted them, and therefore pose a potential threat to the survival of that community.

Survival of the Human Race

Chapter 10: Governments

"Of the people, by the people, and for the people..."

There are many types of governments in power today. They range from people having a high degree of freedom to people having relatively little. How do these governments gain power, and how do they maintain it? What is the ideal government? Is there such a thing?

As nations decay, new ones replace them. The process of forming a new government is sometimes an easy, gradual transition; sometimes it is drastic and often it fails. Governments are able to stay in power either by having the approval of the people or control of the people. The former simply means that the people have some control over the government and have some say in its actions. The latter means that the government has control over most of the people, and is able to remain in power because of this control, whether most people like it or not. Of course this may be an extreme, but such governments do exist today.

Just as we looked at relationships within a community, relationships that support survival of governments must be built on integrity and allegiance. No matter what form of government is in power, it is our hypothesis that their leaders must act with these qualities as their backbone to survive in the long term.

Survival of the Human Race

Democracy Versus Dictatorship

In the U.S. we hear a great deal about the benefits of democracy over dictatorship. What are these benefits? If one takes the time to look up the definition of democracy in different texts and dictionaries, one finds significant differences in definition. We found it difficult to come up with a simple definition. In fact, different governments that call themselves "democracies" have considerably different structures and voting rights. Some basic attributes that are typically expounded as being characteristic of democracy are the following:

- One man, one vote;

- The government is of the people, by the people, and for the people;

- The officials who control the government, particularly taxation and spending, are elected by all the people;

- All of the residents over a prescribed age are eligible to vote.

These "obvious" characteristics are not directly characteristic of many democracies. We will start by considering just who among the people (of the allowed voting age) are *really* allowed to vote. One may naturally think that all residents can vote. Well, most countries restrict voting to those who are deemed *citizens*. So what does it take to be a citizen? In the U.S., if you are born here, you are a citizen. You can also become a citizen by naturalization, i.e., through immigration, sponsorship, obtaining a working permit, and years as a permanent resident. This is not true everywhere and eligibility for citizenship in a nation can make a huge difference. Much of the time it goes unnoticed by the outside world.

Democracies currently exist where large numbers of residents - who were born there - have no vote. In some cases, eligible voters have been forcibly driven out of their homeland - where they were born and have lived for generations, so that a minority can take power. Some people have been paid bounties to migrate into a country - to move voting control into the hands of an otherwise political minority.

Survival of the Human Race   78

Some democracies allow (even encourage) dual citizenship, allowing residents to vote in two countries. Dual citizenship leads to questions of allegiance and conflicts of interest. As President George W. Bush said when he declared war on terrorism in 2001, "You are either with us, or against us!" One must make a choice. When forced to make a decision to help one nation versus the other, where does one's allegiance lie? The truth must be stated up front. Else allegiance is in question, and the underpinnings of democracy can become undermined.

We don't want the wrong impression to be taken by our discussion of democracy. We believe readers should have the facts, and encourage them to learn the true situation before taking pronouncements at face value. We believe that the kind of democracy existing in the U.S. is reasonably good, especially compared to most dictatorships. We think there are important underlying reasons why democracy tends to be fair for all the people who live here, not just its citizens. We are trying to paint the true picture, that is - *forms of democracy vary widely.*

Dictatorships are somewhat easier to define. In a dictatorship the dictator has power and authority over the people. Dictators usually have some form of advisement council and governing staff. Depending upon the dictator, their council and staff, the people may have little say in what the government does. The dictator may make all the decisions regardless of what the people want. Of course, such a dictator is subject to being overthrown. History is replete with coups and overthrown dictators. Some of these have been very nasty and bloody, where people end up voting with their swords.

Many governments lie somewhere in between. Some republics may look like dictatorships, in which the people only get to vote at the lowest level of government. If this form of government was present in the U.S., the people would only vote for municipal-level officials. The elected officials at the municipal level would then vote for the next level, e.g., the county officials. The county officials would then vote for the state officials, and the state officials would vote for the Federal officials, a pyramid type voting scheme.

Survival of the Human Race

In this form of government, there is no direct vote for the Federal officials. Russia and China are examples of republics with variations on these forms of government. One can argue the fairness of elections, but that is a completely different matter, just as was argued in the U.S. 2000 Presidential Election in Florida. Fairness of elections is a separate issue - not to be confused with the type of government.

Recognition of Freedom and Privacy

We hold the firm opinion that freedom and privacy are the most important characteristics of any government. Protecting private ownership of property - *particularly the land* - is the most essential ingredient of a fair government. If the people do not own the land, they cannot control the government. This implies a legal system that (1) upholds and protects private ownership, with the ability of owners to transfer that ownership as they see fit, and (2) adjudicates disputes on a fair basis. China now recognizes this principle, and is fast becoming a world superpower because of it. Russia is finally starting to take these steps, after watching China race by.

Why is private ownership so important? Are we advocating Barons and Earls? Absolutely not! The more dispersed the ownership the better. In our opinion, this is why the U.S. has become the world's most formidable superpower. A very large segment of the U.S. voting population consists of landowners, homeowners, and business property owners.

Having a large percentage of the population owning land and homes is essential to the people's ability to exercise power over a government. We believe it inevitably leads to *real* democracy. Those who own land (and homes) are more likely to have a real interest in their politicians' behavior. Landowners are more likely to keep politicians aware of the public concerns and ensure their allegiance. Whether or not politicians choose to embrace the concerns of their constituents, or the concerns of special and conflicting interests, will likely affect their ability to get re-elected.

Survival of the Human Race

This conflict between the people's interests and politician's actions is a constant fight for budgetary control and the power to make and interpret laws. How do the people know that the politician they are voting for will act with their best interests in mind? Once politicians are elected, they have ultimate control over what decisions are made within their position. This is a very powerful position. So what about the power of the people?

Power Of People Versus Politicians

Do politicians really have that much power? They aren't very powerful when faced with fair elections. In order to get elected time and time again, if the position allows, they must keep their constituents happy and look out for their interests. If they don't do this, then it is likely that people will be voting for someone else next term.

Along with knowing what the people want, politicians also keep in mind their own interests and agendas. Politicians have personal interests that they want put into policy, that's why they are in politics! There are ways to push for their constituents' interests while integrating their own interests into legislation. For some politicians this is extremely easy because their interests parallel those of their constituents. In other cases, this is very tricky work, but it is done often. If politicians are in a position to grant certain favors, they can manipulate substantial power. They can influence powerful organizations, such as unions, religious organizations, and the media. Some politicians are highly skilled at deception, and even at changing the voting process, particularly the definition of who can vote for them. Gerrymandering, immigration, and voting rights are examples of this.

So how can we, the people, be sure that even though politicians are integrating their interests with ours, they are still keeping our best interests out in front? Is there a way to be sure? If we don't seek out the truth, learn all about a politicians motives, and ensure their allegiance, we take a high risk.

Survival of the Human Race

The people must be both encouraged and able to seek the truth for themselves, and not rely on information given to them from sources that are politically biased. Information from biased sources only serves to influence a person's thoughts about the subject, as opposed to providing real information to help make fair decisions. To avoid being swayed unfairly by biased inputs, we must search out as many sources as we can - to be sure we gain the "unshakable facts."

With this knowledge at our disposal, we are more apt to recognize when someone passes biased information. We are in a better position to know who is being truthful and who is being deceitful. This is very powerful information to have when it comes to our government. It is a good feeling to know whom we can trust!

In this type of democracy, power can be in the people's hands, and government must act accordingly. This power of knowledge can work wonders to ensure fairness, heighten the competitive levels, and ensure excellence in a country.

Fair Competition

Politicians are constantly competing with one another to get ahead in the race for office. In an environment where people work hard to seek the truth, politicians will be forced to prove their integrity and allegiance. Putting them into a competition for candidacy helps to weed out bad candidates and bring about healthy competition. By having "fair competition" during a campaign, we mean competition that revolves around issues, not personal attacks on the candidate. Instead of having to worry about "whom" we are voting for - as in a beauty or popularity contest - we will be able to consider "what" we are voting for. We can think about the issues at hand, what issues are most important to us, and who has the best policy to resolve them favorably. All this is brought about through fair competition, and fair competition is brought about when the citizens seek the truth without prejudice.

Survival of the Human Race

With fair competition, we may be able to put people who are honest and considerate in high positions. We need leaders with allegiance to their constituents and nation, leaders who keep the people in mind, not other agendas such as personal gain.

Haves Versus Have-Nots

To garner more votes, politicians typically play on the disparity between the "haves versus have-nots." Since fifty percent of the people in any population are below average by any measure, it is easy to appeal to a large percentage of a population by telling them that they are unfairly put below average. Anyone below average enjoys hearing that it is not their fault, and that they are up against unfair odds. This generally works since, by definition, fifty percent of the people in any population are below average. Of course, their inherent problems may never be solved, but it provides hope, and it is possible for people to change places. And most important - it can get votes.

Referring back to Figure 7-1, if we start with population A, and work to improve everyone's ability to compete, we can achieve the results of population B in the distribution. Note that as everyone improves, everyone moves up the scale. In fact, a majority of the people that were in the lower half of the A distribution are now well above the average that existed before the change. As John Kennedy said when justifying his tax cuts in the early 1960s, "A rising tide lifts all boats." So everyone should be happy, right? Not necessarily so.

In looking at the distribution in B, everyone has improved substantially. But the disparity between the people at the top end of the scale and those at the bottom has grown. They are further apart. And this is what politicians play on. On a relative basis, things appear to have gotten worse. In a fair competitive environment, the hard workers will move further ahead than those at the lower end, and this is always noticeable, even though everyone is doing better than before.

Unfortunately, this very positive outcome also allows politicians to point to the larger disparity - to counter the positive results. This appeals to people who do not want to compete. This is the main attraction of socialism and communism, where everyone is *supposed* to be *equal*. Of course, if you have the right political friends or position, you can always be *more equal*.

Fiscal Responsibility

We have a huge government in the U.S. with many large departments and sub-organizations, each with many high paying positions to be filled. These departments, such as Defense, State, Homeland Security, etc., contract with private sources for goods and services to support their operations. The government also doles out huge amounts of money to various other nations around the world. Much of this money is used under agreement with these nations to buy goods and services from U.S. contractors and manufacturers. Needless to say, people making the decisions on expenditures are in very powerful positions. Who pays for all these jobs, purchases, and contracts? Where does all the money come from? The answer is: from the U.S. taxpayers.

Taxpayers ultimately give their *own* money to pay for the U.S. Federal government's expenses. These expenses amount to trillions of dollars every year, a number so large, that the average person cannot relate to it. As we can see from Figure 8-1, government spending is increasing. What is worse, the private sector's share of the economy is decreasing. Are the politicians spending the money the way they should? Or are they just buying votes? Why is the U.S. government growing relative to the private sector, while the governments of some of our so-called communist friends, e.g., China and Russia, are doing the reverse? Are we trading places?

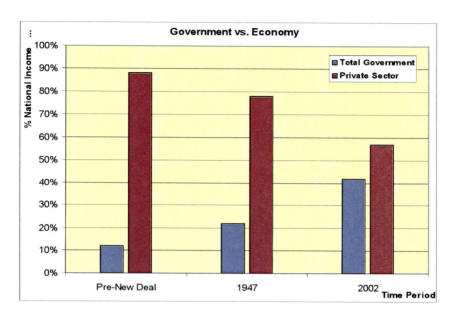

Figure 8-1 Government spending versus the economy.[1]

Let's consider the rudiments of the Federal government's budgetary process. Every year each government agency proposes its *fiscal budget*. This is rolled up and approved by the congress and the president. When the government spends more money than the annual income can support, it is called a budget deficit. A deficit occurs when the money spent is in excess of the income that year. Figure 8-2 shows the government deficits in the period from 1928 through 2008. Except for small periods before 1968, the government has been spending much more than it takes in for many years, with the worst being since 2003. What would happen if taxpayers did this? As measured by their balance sheets, they would be broke - in bankruptcy! In fact, many small municipalities publish an audited balance sheet so the voters can see where they stand financially. They too would be in bankruptcy with no ability to sell bonds. People overseeing the Federal Government balance sheet interpret it differently. So what's the truth?

Survival of the Human Race

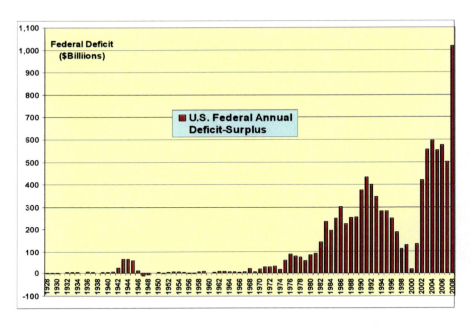

Figure 8-2 Government deficits from 1928 to 2008.[2]

To run a deficit, the government has to borrow money. The sum of the deficits that the government has accumulated from year to year is the Federal (National) debt. Figure 8-3 shows the national debt and its relation to the interest on the public debt for the years 1928-2008. The national debt after the fiscal year 2008 was over $10 trillion.[3] As U.S. Federal government spending increases, so does the *national debt*.

Since the taxpayers are the only ones who can pay off the debt, how can the U.S. ever expect to pay off its debt if the Federal budget keeps growing at the current rate? Taxpayers will be expected to give more and more money to the government as the national debt increases to an exorbitant amount. Interest rates have been very low over the past few years. If they are allowed to rise, the interest on the *debt* will be a major annual expense, a typical cause for destruction of the currency and bankruptcy.

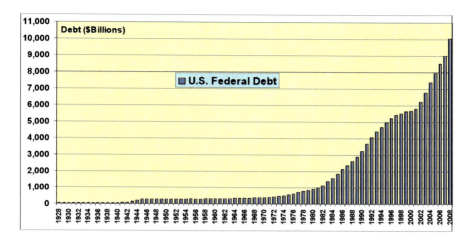

Figure 8-3 U.S. Federal (National) Debt.[4]

In 1816, Thomas Jefferson said that he placed "economy among the first and most important of republican virtues, and *debt as the greatest of the dangers* to be feared."[5] This implies that the people who pay for the government have control over the spending. In other words, the politicians who make decisions on expenditures must decrease spending in order to decrease the national debt. But this hasn't happened - at least in the last 40 years. We must ask -Why is it getting worse faster? It is clearly out of control!

There is no way to decrease the deficit except to cut spending or increase taxes. At some point, it's going to require the politicians to cut back on spending programs. So why aren't the politicians held accountable? Because this is a truth that the majority of people do not want to hear. Most people feel that, as long as the other guy is paying, it is OK! So who is the other guy?

Some people consider the U.S. Federal government a lender of last resort. Why would someone crown our government with this title? Maybe it's because the politicians are constantly willing to buy people's votes.

If we think about this more carefully, we will see that the politicians are not using government money. They are using *taxpayer* money. The taxpayers are the lenders of the last resort! As William Weld said, *"There is no such thing as government money - only taxpayer money."*[6]

Who Pays The Taxes?

So who are the taxpayers? Looking at the top curve (red) in Figure 8-4, of the US people that file tax returns, approximately 1% pay more than 35% of the taxes, 5% pay 55% of the taxes while 25% pay more than 80% of the taxes.[7,8] The majority of people (51%) who do pay taxes contribute less than 5% of the tax revenue. The bottom curve (black) shows people on a 1 percentile basis, assuming everyone in the same bracket pays the same taxes. Again we note that this chart does *not* include anyone *not* filing tax returns.

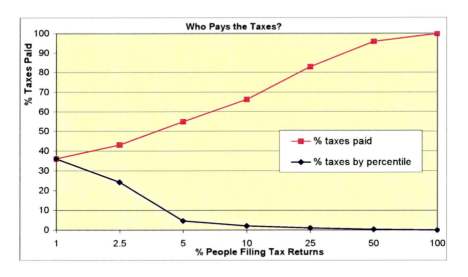

Figure 8-4. Distribution of Federal taxes over the population.[9]

Besides considering who is paying the taxes, we should know who is spending the money and how. The taxpayers should know where their money is going. After all, it is their money the government is spending! Some people generally know where some of it goes, but not all of it. So where does all this money go?

Politicians seem to be out buying votes - all the time, instead of solving real fiscal problems. When politicians begin to dole out favors to large groups of people using taxpayer money (to get a large block of votes), we lose fair and honest taxpayer representation.

Taxpayers should try to understand what they are paying for. Besides wanting to know where the Federal government spends their money, taxpayers should know their proportion of voter representation. Are the taxpayers fairly represented? Some people claim that there is "taxation without representation" in the U.S. today. If a majority of voters pay only a small portion of the taxes, how can taxpayers ever expect to be fairly represented? How can this happen?

Taxpayer Representation

We have not acquired data on the dollar amount of taxes paid by population distribution. But the important point that can be derived from the above data in Figure 8-4 is that 50% of the people filing tax returns are paying less than 5% of the taxes. We do not know what percent of the voting population file tax returns, but it is certainly less than 100%. In addition, some percentage of taxpayers do not vote. Therefore, we believe it is quite safe to say that a majority of the voters pay less than 5% of the taxes. Is this fair representation?

Let's consider a system where everyone of voting age paid exactly the same amount of tax. This would require everyone to pay on the order of $10,000 in Federal taxes to match the current Federal government revenues. This would be a true *flat tax*. It would clearly provide a fair representation of voters as taxpayers. Of course, this would be impossible for any politician to sell today considering that 50% of the eligible voters pay only a small percentage of this, if any.

As an alternative, all people of voting age could pay a linearly increasing tax, e.g., 10% of their income (this is improperly called a *flat tax* by politicians). Thus, the more one earns, the more tax one pays. For many people, this is a penalty for working harder and earning more!

It turns out that this is still very hard to sell, because the current tax system is much worse than linear. Taxes go up much faster than "linearly" with earnings. As a result, a major share of the population would still have to pay much higher taxes than they do now. When a majority of the population pays a very small percent of the tax, they want more services. After all, it is not their money. To get elected, politicians must keep promising more to these people to get their votes. The fact that the country may be going broke is not of interest to them. As long as it is not their money - they don't care.

We must note that people who own real estate pay additional taxes to local, county, and state governments. In many areas of the country, this is a substantial amount. In most small towns, they can stay on top of the politicians and have some control. In larger cities, this is difficult. Similarly for state governments that dip into local property taxes as well as income taxes.

The bottom line of this analysis is that it is currently difficult for those people paying most of the taxes to control the politicians. In fact, without another American Revolution, we do not see how to stop this speeding train before it crashes. And it has to crash because over 50% of the U.S. debt is held by China and the Arabs. If the train crashes, these countries, not liked by our politicians, are left holding the bag. So who are the winners in this game of Russian Roulette?

The winners are those people who control the money that gets the politicians elected - the so-called *special interest groups*. These people have many ways to translate political contributions into profits. One way or another, they get back large multipliers on their contributions. For example, a $5M contribution may get a $500M return.

Money may come back to them in many ways. It can come in the form of legislation, contracts, grants, and sometimes handouts to foreign countries that are supposed to be our friends and allies.

If one tries to do research on who are the major political contributors, one can find the winners up to about 2004, when political contributions were tracked by the overall organization. After 2004 this becomes difficult. Because of the heat some of these organizations were receiving, they have hidden their contributions behind large numbers of constituent groups, or so called *soft money* contributions such as *free* advertising or the equivalent.

But if one looks hard enough prior to 2004, it is not hard to find the data and plot the curves of increasing contributions by certain organizations, contributions that just drop like a bomb after the changes in approach to contributing and reporting. These contributors are siphoning off huge amounts of taxpayer money and putting it into hidden storage, sometimes offshore.

We want it to be known that we are not advocating one group receiving special attention over others; this is already taking place. We are advocating that all groups gain a fair representation of their interests based upon what they really contribute to the government on a net basis, not the number of votes that they can help get for a candidate.

Survival of the Human Race

* * *

No matter what person or politician we are discussing, we must ensure that they are honest and considerate. If these people have integrity and allegiance, then they will encourage fair competition within our nations. We will also be able to have healthy competition between nations, resolving conflicts in fair ways.

If a democratic society exists where the majority of voters pay little or no taxes, they are probably going to vote for raising taxes on those that do, and increasing spending programs that help themselves. If most voters are in this position, then they aren't concerned about those that pay the taxes, only how much is spent - on themselves. We are not saying that these people should not make their interests known; we are saying that if their interests are overwhelming a minority of the population with unfair taxes while creating huge deficits, we need to reconsider the situation. That's why there was a Boston tea party and an American Revolution!

But all of this is not nearly as bad as being dishonest about running a government that cannot pay its bills - one that must print money to pay the interest on its growing debt. The taxpayers must be fairly represented. Otherwise, they will be looted by politicians and their benefactors, who buy votes from those who do not pay their fair share, so they can all stay in power. And when the train crashes, these deceitful people will still be the winners.

For a nation to secure its survival, the people must learn and understand what goes on inside the government, where the money goes, and who has control over the supply. We must ensure that the power rests with the people who are paying the bills, i.e. the real taxpayers, to make certain political power can be seen as fair and honest, not viewed as biased and deceitful.

Survival of the Human Race

Chapter 11: Disputes

"Every story has three sides to it - yours, mine,
and the facts."
- Foster Meharny Russell

When we have disputes with our neighbors or fellow residents, who settles them? In the U.S. we would go to the municipality in which we reside and it would be settled there in a court of law. But what if there are disputes between municipalities?

Disputes between municipalities, are settled at the county level. Disputes between counties go to the state. If there are disputes between states, they are taken to the federal government. Within our nation, disputes can be resolved, for better or worse, for the individuals or organizations involved. But what if there are disputes between national governments?

Disputes Between Nations

Nations have inherent differences in their values and priorities leading to governments with different agendas. Each national government has its own nation's interests at stake and gains in mind. Sometimes the interests of different nations are in conflict. When different governments walk onto the international playing field, these conflicting interests may bring about major disputes.

Survival of the Human Race

Some of the more common disputes are over territory, natural resources, trade, etc. These vast assets are important to all nations, and each nation has their individual perspective on them. Different national ideals tend to conflict, and disagreements occur frequently. The evidence is apparent from any newspaper, radio, or TV program covering international news.

With so many disputes between nations, we must be concerned about how and where they can be resolved. In fact, various international organizations have been formed by many groups of countries with the purpose of settling such disputes. As prime examples, most nations on our planet who wished to participate in such an organization became part of the League of Nations or, its replacement, the United Nations. These international organizations were formed to provide a forum to help settle disputes between countries. So what's the history? How have they faired?

The League of Nations

The League of Nations was an international organization created in 1919 after WWI as part of the Treaty of Versailles. It started with 42 member nations. The League was created to promote international cooperation and achieve international peace and security. States who signed the Covenant were required to submit disputes between them to this organization before going to war.

Concurrent with and for a short period after its creation, the few powers that helped to create it were in a position to wield their influence. Some nations used this international body to achieve national goals. This was before the many additional nations that joined could use their influence to create an environment that was considered fair to them all.

Eventually, the body gained wide support and participation; its highest number of member states was 58 in 1934. As time went on, the League helped to prevent small wars and, through cooperation of states, brought about a collective consciousness of international affairs.

As the League of Nations grew in membership, key nations were no longer able to wield influence for national purposes. To be more blunt, they could not accomplish their obvously unfair objectives when so many other nations were watching. This caused consternation, and the League eventually began losing members. In 1942 the last country to withdraw did so leaving the League with only 44 members until its demise. If one searches out the true history, it becomes clear that some nations advocated the demise of the League of Nations because they no longer could use their influence as they did when the body was new. With the onset of WWII, the assets of the League of Nations were turned over to the newly created United Nations.[1]

The United Nations

The same powers that helped to create the League of Nations helped to create the United Nations (UN). The UN was formally organized in 1945, with 51 Member States, taking the place of the League of Nations. Again, concurrent with and for a short period after its creation, these same powers were in a position to wield their influence. Some of these nations used this international body to quickly achieve national goals. This was before the additional nations got on board and started to diffuse the influence.

Today, the UN contains 191 Member States, a huge increase. This organization tries to secure international peace and cooperation among participating countries. The UN maintains international organizations, such as the International Telecommunication Union, under its umbrella as specialized agencies.[2]

Survival of the Human Race

The UN attempts to give protection to its member states. When there are disputes, the UN attempts to take all factors into consideration to come up with a fair resolution. When nations have territorial disputes with others and need the help of a body like the UN, the UN can act as a liaison and bring the two nations together to help come to an agreement.

The UN also helps out nations that are struggling with problems such as disease, poverty, or natural disasters. The UN helps these nations by lending money, supplies, and assistance. It helps nations in need to increase their chance of survival.

The UN is also taking strides to become a loose "governing" body. Members have developed a system of international laws that "play a central role in promoting economic and social development, as well as international peace and security."[3] Some of these laws are already in existence, such as international criminal law and international environmental law, while others are still being discussed, such as outer space law and law of the sea. There also exists an International Court of Justice.

But at the onset of the new millennium, one has to wonder if the same demise that occurred with the League of Nations will occur again with the UN. Certain nations that can no longer wield their influence and deceive their fellow members are bashing the UN just as they bashed the League of Nations. Will key nations pull out because they cannot wield their influence for national purposes? But why would anyone want to dismantle the UN today? Is it better to start over again, trying to create a fair body of people who represent their nations? Will starting over put us ahead - or behind?

In the end, it all comes down to seeking the truth. And this depends on the people who control the decisions and policies in their respective nations. It is the people who control the organization that make it a success or failure. In the case of the U.N., it is those politicians controlling the nations that contribute the most money that wield the most influence. Will they follow the wrong golden rule? ("He who has the gold rules!")

Survival of the Human Race

To make the UN a success, one must address the problems of conflicts of interest and allegiance. The UN cannot be concerned with what goes on inside national borders, but what goes on between nations when one nation comes to it for adjudication. How can a body at the international level settle disputes *between* nations in an unbiased way to gain a fair outcome? How can we create distinct laws and rules to make sure fairness and trust are preserved?

People with unquestionable integrity must represent the nations. Although one may be dealing with others to whom there is no allegiance, consideration must still prevail. Nations must reciprocate truth and consideration. Simply put, they must follow the *real* golden rule: "do onto others as you would have them do unto you." If the focus of disputes is based upon judgments of member behavior with respect to their integrity and consideration of their fellow nations, deception should be eliminated and friendship should prevail.

Finally, the UN has developed a significant infrastructure with many relations, organizations, and links throughout the world. What can be gained from tearing this down and starting over? What nations will gain and what nations will lose by dismantling the UN? Is there a systemic problem here? If so, building a new infrastructure will not solve the real problem. It could be used to unfair advantage - for the third time. This problem should be addressed in an open media forum, with the existing infrastructure. Seeking and exposing the truth - to as many people around the world as possible - is the best way to resolve this issue. It is clearly unfair to allow a few unhappy nations to bring about the demise of the UN. We should determine what the *real* underlying problems are, secure what we already have created, and work to make it better.

It is our belief that the kinds of achievements made by the UN in its efforts to gain peace and security in our world should continue. Many people are working at the UN everyday to reduce the threat of terrorism and other forms of threats to the human race. Clearly the major threat that exists today is not terrorism. It is the nuclear threat, which has been addressed by the UN since its start.

Survival of the Human Race

Unfortunately, exposure of the real nuclear threats in the world appears not in the best interests of certain influential nations. As a result, this most important issue is kept from being addressed fairly. Could the fact that fairness is not in the best interests of all nations be the problem with the UN? If so, starting a new world body will not solve this most basic problem. It will only help those nations who benefit from hiding the truth to prolong unfairness. Is this a case of history getting ready to repeat itself?

The Nuclear Threats

Nuclear weapons are clearly the major threat to the world today. At least 8 countries have them, and many more are suspected to be in the process of developing them. If such weapons (of real mass destruction) get into the wrong hands, our survival is clearly at stake. And when we say "we", we mean everyone on planet earth.

What protection do we have against nuclear weapons? One protection the UN has tried to create is the Treaty on the Non-Proliferation of Nuclear Weapons (NPT). The NPT is considered "the most widely accepted arms control agreement." It obligates those states that sign it as follows: States that have nuclear weapons are not allowed to transfer to another any such weapons, technology, or information that pertains to nuclear technology in general. It also requires that states that don't have nuclear weapons not acquire or produce any nuclear explosive devices. Furthermore, "any nuclear materials in peaceful civil facilities under the jurisdiction of the state must be declared to the International Atomic Energy Agency (IAEA), whose inspectors have routine access to the facilities for periodic monitoring and inspections."[4]

As of today, 187 states are Parties to the NPT. Of the states that are considered nuclear powers with a large store of weapons, only one has not signed this treaty.[5] Two others, known to have some small nuclear capability, have not signed this treaty. Why won't all nations sign this treaty?

Survival of the Human Race

The UN and its NPT is clearly a source of protection and a forum to bring nations together to achieve a fair understanding of what's best for human survival. But is this sufficient protection? Why should any countries possess nuclear weapons that can be used outside their borders. We must work to ensure that this significant nuclear dilemma is resolved peacefully before there is any use of these weapons.

Possession of nuclear weapons is clearly the number one problem with regard to survival of the human race. It is not the organization of the UN that is preventing the solution of this problem. It is those nations that refuse to open up their doors - to reveal the truth and to cooperate - that are the problem. This situation must be dealt with internationally, by revealing it to the world. We believe that the UN is the best place to do it, with all the nations of the world looking on. Why would anyone want to keep this from happening?

* * *

While there are many disputes in the world today, individual nations need the protection of a world body to help ensure their security. This is especially true for nations without significant military power, and particularly true for those without nuclear weapons. We must make sure that such an organization emphasizes critical values, such as integrity and consideration, among its members. Such an international body must seek the truth to be able to make fair decisions. Members must be able to tell the truth, without fear of reprisal, so that all of the people in the member nations can have access to the facts.

We must address problems of conflict of interest and allegiance. Within the UN, and particularly with those states having nuclear capabilities, we must determine where allegiances lie and where conflicts of interest exist. The world needs protection by fair and unbiased decision makers, and strong action against any resistance to truth and fairness.

Survival of the Human Race

With the horrific impasse of the nuclear era, it is our position that the UN must stay out in front of the opposition in our fight for survival. All people, as individuals, must ensure that nations who would wield their power unfairly, to gain a better position with regard to their neighbors, are held in abeyance, and particularly from destroying the single body of nations that has been put together to protect us all. It is our responsibility as individual citizens, of every nation on earth, to ensure the survival of the United Nations and the human race as far into the future as we can control.

Chapter 12: Conclusion

"In time of war the first casualty is truth."
-Boake Carter

With our world in an era of vast quantities of extremely powerful nuclear weapons, we must take every possible step to ensure our survival. We must inform ourselves about everything that is going on around us. Most of all, we must make sure that the information we are getting is factual and unbiased. This is particularly true when trying to obtain international news where, in the U.S., most people can only receive news from syndicated networks, networks that depend upon politicians for broadcast licenses.

We must establish and maintain good relationships with people in our communities, from the smallest municipality to the largest nations. We must support the protection of private property to ensure our communities won't decay. We must ensure our leaders are honest and considerate, and that their allegiance is with their community. With such leaders in office, our government will encourage fair competition. With private property ownership and fair competition, the power will rest in the hands of the people and democracy will be an inevitable result - instead of an issue. We must keep fiscal affairs out in the open instead of behind closed doors, and ensure that the real taxpayers control where their money goes. We must remember that the American Revolution was motivated by taxation without representation.

Information is power, and if we have it, we have the ability to throw up flags and ask questions. Through demands for accurate history, and the use of measurement and science, we can situate truth and allegiance with high integrity. Since history is about our past, we must work to ensure that it is accurate and told without bias. The same goes for the present. The media can best help by presenting unbiased, factual information to the public - instead of pushing agendas. This will ensure that our knowledge is based upon a foundation of truth, facts and honest measurements.

Using distributions we can measure and expose the real differences within a society accurately. But the distribution measures must be based upon facts. Scientific facts are proven to be true only through the use of scientific methods. With these tools we can gain truth and facts, and a prolonged life for our most cherished communities. Given the use of these tools, we can apply the concepts of integrity and allegiance to our everyday lives.

Truth is a subject that everyone needs to fully understand. We must demand the truth when we are seeking it and use integrity when we are telling it. We must make sure that we are surrounded by the whole truth, and not be blinded by biased perceptions of it.

Along with this comes the importance of allegiance which is also a form of consideration. It is based upon the real Golden Rule. Not only do we need to have allegiance towards our country, but we need to consider allegiance in every aspect of our lives. We must apply these principles with our friends, family, work, communities, etc. We must avoid conflicts of interest, such as when people are disloyal and deceptive. Understanding these concepts will definitely enhance our chances for survival.

We must learn how to survive on earth with the population growing fast. With more people using limited resources, survival becomes important. Understanding our concepts of integrity and allegiance, our chance for survival increases significantly.

Survival of the Human Race

We can prolong survival by settling disputes fairly, building trustworthy and considerate relationships between governments, and maintaining thriving relationships within our communities around the world. We must observe what goes on in our world through unbiased history, accurate measurement, and exposition of the true facts. By maintaining truth, consideration, and allegiance in all of the above aspects, we will help to ensure our survival.

Our motivation for writing this book is to help people gain the knowledge necessary to ensure survival of the human race. We would like all people to gain the ability to look into the future with a clear vision, and to be able to navigate their own lives toward safe and sound environments. This implies being willing to seek out the truth and able to overcome obstacles that may reduce their likelihood of survival.

As we stated in the introduction, the survivors will be those who have the desire to seek the truth and expose it with integrity. They will be prepared to make the hard decisions, exert the energy to change direction, and invoke the self-discipline to improve their likelihood of survival. They will be the ones who gain the knowledge of how to survive and have the courage to use it.

We thank you for reading our book, and will greatly appreciate any comments that you may have to help in our quest to prolong the survival of the human race.

Survival of the Human Race

References

Introduction:

1. Hersch, Seymour, The Sampson Option, Random House, New York, 1991.

Chapter 1:

1. Levy, Steven, Artificial Life, Random House, New York, 1993.

Chapter 2:

1. Glazer, Jack, "This is Your Brain on Bias - Perception, Memory, and Unintended Discrimination," Fifth Annual Symposium on Fairness & Equity, April 1992.
2. Schlesinger, Arthur M. Jr., The Disuniting of America. W. W. Norton & Company: New York, 1992. pp.52.
3. Geneen, Harold. Managing. Avon Books: New York, 1984. pp. 101-102, 122.
4. Ibid.

Chapter 3:

1. Hersch, Seymour, The Sampson Option, Random House, New York, 1991.

Chapter 4:

1. O'Brien, Patrick K., ed. Atlas of World History. George Philip Limited: USA, 1999.
2. Winckler, Suzanne and Rodgers, Mary M. Our Endangered Planet: Population Growth. Lerner Publications Company: Minneapolis, 1991.

Chapter 5:

1. "Pledge of Allegiance." American tees. February 2, 2004.
   http://www.americantees.com/pledge_of_allegiance.htm.
2. Schlesinger. pp.35.

Chapter 6:

1. Schlesinger. pp.46.
2. Ibid.
3. Mettler, Ruben. "Cargo Cult Mentality in America,"
   Business Week Magazine, September 22, 1980. p. 22
4. Ibid.
5. Ibid.
6. Schlesinger, Chapter 4: pp. 45

Chapter 8:

1. Rueff, Jacques. "The Fallacies of Lord Keynes' General Theory,"
   Quarterly Journal of Economics. May 1947, pp.343

Chapter 9:

1. Shevardnadze, Eduard. The Future Belongs to Freedom.
   The Free Press: NY, 1991. pp.24.
2. Ibid.

Chapter 10:

1. Grandfather Economic Report Summary by M W Hodges.
   March 11, 2004. http://mwhodges.home.att.net/summary.htm
2. "Budget Explorer: The Complete US Federal Budget"
   January 5, 2005. http://www.kowaldesign.com/budget/.
3. "Debt to the Penny." March 11. 2004.
   http://www.publicdebt.treas.gov/opd/opdpenny.htm.
4. "Budget Explorer: The Complete US Federal Budget"
   January 5, 2005. http://www.kowaldesign.com/budget/.
5. Quoted at http://mwhodges.home.att.net/summary.htm.
6. quoted from Reader's Digest at
   http://mwhodges.home.att.net/summary.htm.

7. "Tax Report: A special summary and forecast of federal and state tax developments." *Wall Street Journal.* February 16, 2002.
8. "Taxes: How the super-rich lucked out twice." *Business Week.* May 14, 2001
9. Data points were taken from the Joint Economic Committee, April 2, 2004. http://www.house.gov/jec/press/2000/10-16-0.htm.

Chapter 11:

1. "League of Nations Photo Collections." February 20, 2004. http://www.Indiana.edu/~league/intro.htm.
2. "UN: *History of the UN.*" February 5, 2004. http://www.un.org/aboutun/history.htm.
3. "UN: *International Law.*" February 5, 2004. http://www.un.org/aboutun/basicfacts/inetlaw.htm.
4. "Nuclear Non-Proliferation Treaty." FAS organization. February 6, 2004. http://www.fas.org/nuke/control/npt/
5. Cirincione, Joseph. <u>Deadly Arsenals: Tracking Weapons of Mass Destruction.</u> Carnegie Endowment for International Peace, Washington, D.C., 2002.